Eyewitness
BASKETBALL

Chicago Bulls
pennant

Chuck Taylor All Stars

NBA championship rings

ATLANTA

PETE MARAVICH
HAWKS' GUARD

Trading card

1950s referee's shirt

Original Celtics uniform, 1920s

Tim Duncan

Sue Bird

Eyewitness
BASKETBALL

Written by
JOHN HAREAS

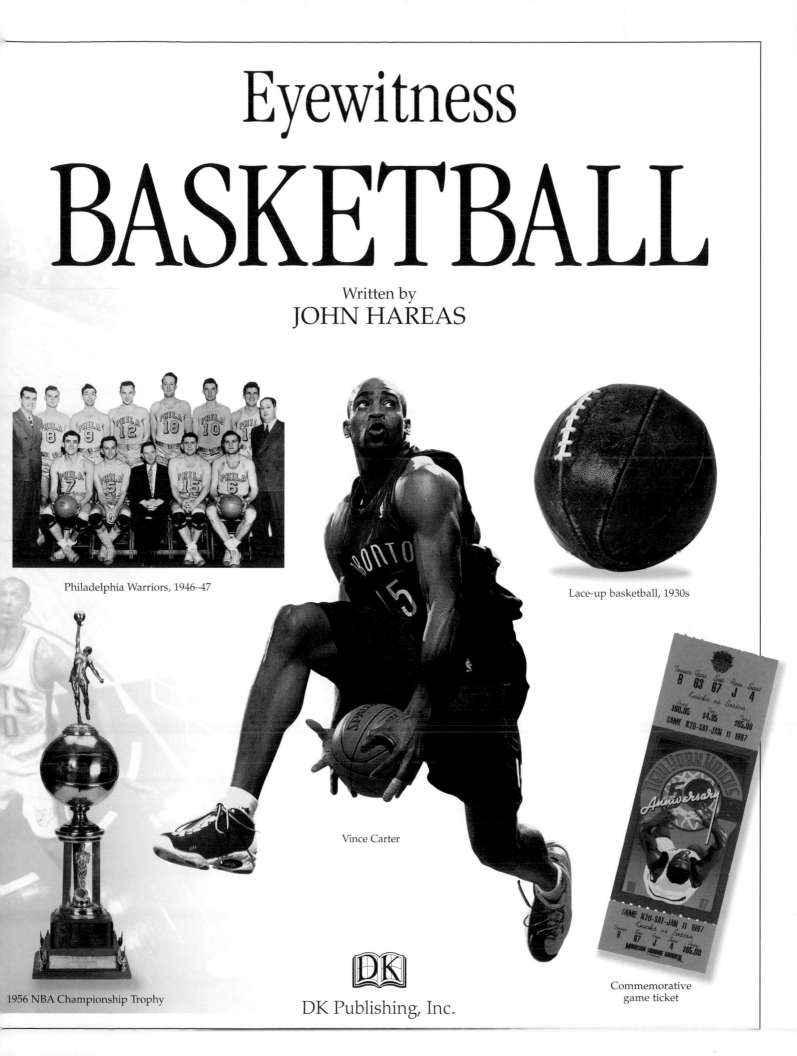

Philadelphia Warriors, 1946–47

Lace-up basketball, 1930s

Vince Carter

1956 NBA Championship Trophy

Commemorative
game ticket

DK

DK Publishing, Inc.

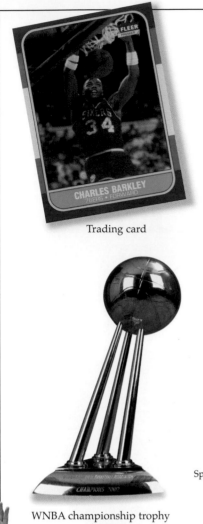

Trading card

DK

LONDON, NEW YORK, MUNICH, MELBOURNE, and DELHI

Publisher Chuck Lang
Project Editor Elizabeth Hester
Assistant Managing Art Editor Michelle Baxter
Creative Director Tina Vaughan
Production Manager Chris Avgherinos
DTP Coordinator Milos Orlovic

REVISED EDITION
Editors Elizabeth Hester, James Buckley, Jr.
Publishing director Beth Sutinis
Art director Dirk Kaufman
DTP designer Milos Orlovic
Production Chris Avgherinos, Ivor Parker

NBA Publishing Charles Rosenzweig, Mario Argote, John Hareas,
Michael Levine, David Mintz, Margaret Williams
NBA Entertainment Photos Carmin Romanelli, Joe Amati, David Bonilla,
Pam Costello, Mike Klein, John Kristofick, Bennett Renda,
Brian Choi, Scott Yurdin
NBA Entertainment Adam Silver, Gregg Winik, Paul Hirschheimer,
Marc Hirschheimer, Rob Sario, Tony Stewart
Photo Editor Joe Amati
Writer John Hareas
NBA Entertainment Staff Photographers Andrew D. Bernstein, Nathaniel S. Butler,
Jesse D. Garrabrant, Jennifer Pottheiser, Steven Freeman

Produced by Shoreline Publishing Group, LLC
Editorial Director James Buckley, Jr.
Designer Thomas J. Carling, Carling Design, Inc.
Revised Edition Designer Diana Catherines, Design Design

Special thanks to the fourth and fifth grade (2001–02) students, and librarian Diane Burkhart-
Kiss of Washington-Hoyt Elementary School in Tacoma, Washington.

This edition published in the United States in 2005
by DK Publishing, Inc.
375 Hudson Street, New York, NY 10014

05 06 07 08 09 10 9 8 7 6 5 4 3 2 1

Hareas, John.
    Basketball / by John Hareas.-- 1st American ed.
    p. cm. -- (Eyewitness)
    Includes index.
    Summary: Text and detailed photographs present the history, techniques, and interesting
    facts of basketball.
    ISBN 0-7566-1063-X (hc) -- 0-7566-1064-8 (alb.)
    ISBN-13: 978 0 7566 1063 0   ISBN-10: 0 7566 1063 X (plc)
    ISBN-13: 978 0 7566 1064 7   ISBN-10: 0 7566 1064 8 (alb)
    1. Basketball--Juvenile literature. 2. National Basketball Association--Juvenile literature.
    [1. Basketball. 2. National Basketball Association.] I. Title. II. Series: DK eyewitness books.
GV885.1.H37 2003
796.323--dc21
                                                2003051457
Color reproduction by
Colourscan, Singapore
Printed in China by Toppan Printing Co.,
(Shenzhen) Ltd.

Discover more at
www.dk.com

Kevin McHale

Original 24-second clock

Allen Iverson "Celebriduck"

WNBA championship trophy

Coach Pat Riley

Contents

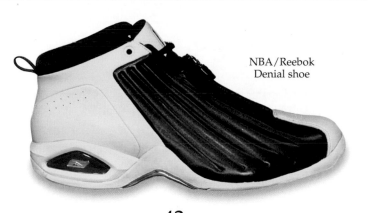

NBA/Reebok
Denial shoe

Beginnings

JAMES NAISMITH WAS AN INSTRUCTOR at the International YMCA Training School in Springfield, Massachusetts, when he was given the assignment that would make him famous: Create an indoor game to help college students pass the time during the long, cold New England winter. In 1891, using a soccer ball, a peach basket, and an empty gym, Naismith invented a game he called "basket ball"—the only major sport created by one person. On an indoor court, teams tried to score points by throwing a ball through a basket nailed to the wall. The game soon grew in popularity, with early teams "barnstorming" from town to town, playing local teams for one night, then moving on to the next city.

Leather lacing

Early basketballs were made of leather panels sewn together.

THE INNOVATORS
They are basketball's pioneers—18 men who played in Dr. Naismith's (center) very first game held in the YMCA gymnasium in Springfield. William Chase (third from left, bottom row) scored the only basket in the historic contest, which ended 1-0.

Naismith used a peach basket nailed to the wall of the YMCA gym as the first "goal."

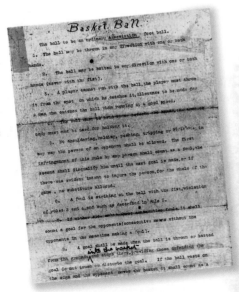

RULES OF "BASKET BALL"
"The object of the game is to put the ball into your opponent's goal," wrote Naismith. The original 13 rules fit onto two pages. Today's rulebook is 60-pages long.

Wires suspended from the walls and ceiling held cages.

THE CAGERS
To play basketball in the early 1900s, you had to be tough. To keep players from falling into the seats, games were played in cages made of chicken wire or steel mesh. Players would often get cut during these intense games. Rope mesh cages (left) eventually came along to the delight of players everywhere.

Sedran played for the Utica (N.Y.) Utes.

Fans sat in folding chairs right next to the action.

Early basketball goals were closed at the bottom. Officials had to get the ball out after each basket.

Canvas shorts

JUMP BALL
The look of the game may have changed, but the basics remain the same. Here, a game in the 1890s begins as modern games do, with a jump ball between two players on opposing teams who try to tap the ball to one of their teammates.

Knee pads

Original Celtics logo

Wool jersey

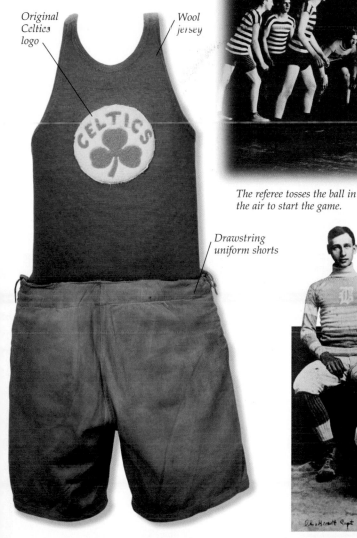

Rubber-soled basketball shoes

MIGHTY MITE
Five-foot, four-inch Barney Sedran earned the nickname the "Mighty Mite of Basketball." The ultra-quick point guard starred in the early 1900s and was one of the era's greatest players. Sedran is the smallest player enshrined in the Hall of Fame.

The referee tosses the ball in the air to start the game.

Players could wear long or short pants

Drawstring uniform shorts

Head coach Dr. Fred Burkhardt

Exposition championship trophy

ORIGINAL NEW YORK CELTICS
The uniform belonged to Ernie Reich of the original Celtics in 1925. The heavy wool jersey and canvas shorts were typical of early uniforms.

THE BUFFALO GERMANS
One of only five complete teams inducted into the Basketball Hall of Fame, the Buffalo Germans once won a staggering 111 straight games. The Germans originated out of a YMCA on Buffalo's East Side in 1895 and compiled a 792–86 record until disbanding in 1925.

PANEL-STYLE BALL
The first basketballs were made of leather panels and resembled soccer balls or volleyballs. Similar versions were used in international competitions until the early 1960s.

Ball and basket

THE BALL FIRST USED BY DR. NAISMITH was a borrowed soccer ball; his net, a wooden basket. Since then, basketball equipment has changed with the game, adapting to advances in technology and new styles of play. Today's pebbled leather ball and flexible nylon net are a far cry from early versions of the ball and basket—but perfectly suited in design and materials to today's fast-paced, high-scoring games.

Raised laces

There are 122 "pebbles" per inch on a basketball.

Orange dye gives the modern basketball its signature color.

Spalding has made the official NBA ball since 1984.

This ball was signed by U.S. President Calvin Coolidge.

LACE-UP BALL
The lace-up ball made its debut in 1894 and lasted into the 1940s. The laces made it difficult to dribble, so players more often used passes to move the ball.

NBA GAME BALL
All NBA balls are made by Spalding Sports Worldwide of Chicopee, Massachusetts. Each ball must follow the same specifications: The circumference must measure between 29 and 29⅞ inches, and the weight must range from 567 to 602 grams. Lastly, each ball must bounce between 52 and 56 inches when dropped from a height of 72 inches.

MADE FOR TV
This yellow-tinted leather ball was used in the 1957 NCAA title game—the first to be televised in color—to help viewers at home locate the ball on TV.

The ABA was active from 1967 until 1976.

THE MAKING OF A BALL
An inflatable bladder made of rubber and nylon string creates the shape of the ball. The thick rubber helps give the ball its high bounce, while the nylon adds durability. After the leather is pressed and tanned, it is printed and bound around the interior layers by rubber seams that help players grip the ball.

Expandable rubber compound

Pebbled leather lining

Each ball has 1.8 miles of nylon winding.

Black rubber bladder

The size and weight of the ball were printed on one panel.

LEAGUE COLORS
This colorful ball was used in the American Basketball Association (ABA). When the ball was thrown, the red, white, and blue panels created a unique kaleidoscope effect.

WNBA logo

THE SMALL BALL
The WNBA basketball was introduced in 1997. It is 2.5 ounces lighter and one inch smaller in diameter than the men's ball. It is made of orange and oatmeal-colored panels.

The evolution of the basket

With the pace of today's games, it's hard to imagine stopping play after each point to retrieve the ball. But high-tech nets and backboards were a long time coming. All sorts of hoops have led the way to the modern basket, and players have adapted to backboards, buzzers, and new materials—and kept shooting for the goal, whatever it looks like.

PEACH BASKET
This is a replica of the peach basket used in Dr. Naismith's first game, in 1891. The two-foot-tall basket featured a closed bottom with a small hole in the center. After each score, a referee would climb a ladder and use a stick to poke the ball out of the basket. This process of retrieving the ball made for a slow game.

Remote-control camera

24-second shot clock counts down to zero, by which time a team must attempt a shot that at least hits the rim.

Time remaining in the quarter is shown here.

These lights turn on to show when time expires.

The shot clock has four sides so it can be seen throughout the arena.

The backboard is made of ½" thick, shatter-resistant glass.

Camera

TRAP-DOOR STYLE
One of the game's early innovations was a trap-door style basket. After each score, the cord attached to the basket was pulled to allow the ball to fall through. The basket itself was made of iron straps.

Movable iron strap flipped down to release the ball.

Cord used to pull down bottom of basket

Padding to protect leaping players

The net is attached to the rim by 12 metal loops.

Nylon netting

Breakaway rim gives slightly under the weight of dunks to prevent damage or injury.

EARLY STRING NET
The first string nets were used in the early 1900s. The "swish" of the net showed whether the ball had passed through the hoop, so devices to trap the ball were no longer needed. The net helped speed up the game.

White box used as a target by players

Early backboards were made of wood.

HOLDING UP THE HOOP
The standard NBA basket and support structure weighs 2,800 pounds and features a backboard, rim, and 24-second shot clock. The colors may change from arena to arena, but the size and shape of NBA goals are always the same: The backboard measures 42 x 72 inches, while the rim is always 18 inches in diameter. Above the backboard, TV or digital cameras are placed on top of the shot clock to give fans a unique view of the action.

Padding at the base of the basket support protects players from injury due to collision.

PLEXIGLASS BACKBOARD
The wooden backboard was introduced in the early 1900s to prevent fans in nearby balcony seats from interfering with shots. In the early 1940s, the plexiglass backboard took its place. The fan-shaped design was created to reduce the size and weight of the larger versions, while allowing fans a better view.

Experimental fan-shaped backboard

The court

BASKETBALL IS PLAYED ON A WOODEN surface called a court that is 94 feet long and 54 feet wide. In the NBA, all courts are made of maple wood, which is very strong, but also flexible to help players jump and land safely. Lines painted on the court define various zones, each with its own purpose and rules. But those are just the facts. What makes a basketball court special is the game that is played on it, the great athletic feats that happen there, and the enjoyment that the game brings to fans.

OLD SCHOOL GAME
Basketball in the 1890s looked very different from today's game. This photo is one of the earliest known showing game action. This game was played outdoors with a basket that lacked a backboard. Today, outdoor courts made of asphalt or concrete are found in every city and town.

Lights signaled a basket scored.

A buzzer sounded at the end of each quarter.

KEEPING TIME
This scoreboard from the 1950s was mounted on a wall above the court so that fans and players could easily see the score and the time remaining in a game. High schools played four eight-minute quarters in those days, which explains the oddly numbered clock. The 1930s "Davis model" controller (below) was used by a courtside scorekeeper to track the score and the time of the game.

Buttons sent signals to the scoreboard.

TALES OF THE HARDWOOD
NBA courts are made of long strips of maple wood connected tightly together. The surface is designed to provide a dependable, even grip and traction to players wearing rubber-soled sneakers or athletic shoes.

The basket at each end is 10 feet from the ground.

Free-throw lane

Foul shots are taken from the free throw line.

The tip-off starts the game at the center circle.

Scores from outside the three-point line earn an extra point.

COURTING GREATNESS
This diagram shows all the lines and zones on an NBA court. (College, high school, and international lines are slightly different.) Each area has a role in the game: The free-throw line is the spot where foul shots are set up. The free-throw lane has a time limit during regular play—players can keep the ball there no more than three seconds before taking a shot. And some of the most exciting shots in the game happen from the three-point line, where players can earn an extra point by scoring from far away. Center circles on pro courts, the site of tip-offs, also include the team logos and colors shown surrounding these two pages.

End line

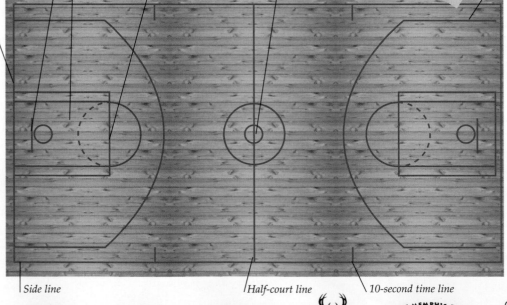

Side line

Half-court line

10-second time line

FAMOUS FLOORING

Perhaps the most unique basketball court floor is the one used by the Celtics at Boston's FleetCenter. Instead of long strips, the floor is made in a traditional checkerboard pattern called "parquet." Workers need about three hours to lay down the 264 panels that make up the floor, plus put up the baskets and courtside seats. Each of the panels is five feet by five feet, and the whole floor is held in place by brass screws and 988 metal bolts.

Stacks of floor panels ready to be laid down

Firm, slightly rubberized sub-surface

The flooring is laid on top of the Boston Bruins' ice-hockey rink.

The free-throw lane area and courtside apron at the Fleet Center are painted Celtics green.

The basket actually hangs three feet over the court, beyond the end line.

WIZARDS

Wheels let players roll the rack anywhere on the court.

BALL RACK

Ball racks like this one are rolled onto the court during pregame warmups. Players can stand next to a rack and shoot many shots from the same spot, grabbing a new ball from the rack each time.

BALL BOYS AND GIRLS: COURT HELPERS

NBA teams employ young ball boys and girls who help out during games. Along with retrieving balls during warm-ups, they are ready with a mop during games to wipe up sweat on the court. They help keep the players safe by preventing slips and falls.

JAZZ

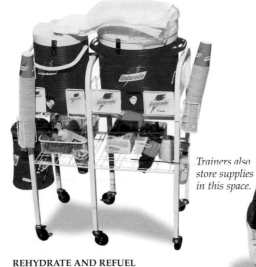

Trainers also store supplies in this space.

RAPTORS

SEATTLE SONICS

REHYDRATE AND REFUEL

Basketball players need to drink plenty of water and sports drinks to keep their bodies ready to play. NBA teams always have a supply of such drinks right at courtside during a game for team members to use.

PRESS ROW

Broadcast and print reporters have some of the best seats in the house. Arena technicians set up computer stations and broadcast equipment right next to the court so reporters can work.

KINGS

NEW ORLEANS HORNETS

NETS

NEW YORK BULLS

Orlando MAGIC

76ERS

PORTLAND BLAZERS

PHOENIX SUNS

SAN ANTONIO SPURS

Referees

THERE ARE 13 PEOPLE ON A COURT DURING A GAME. Ten are the players; the other three are NBA officials, called referees or "refs." Players are required to observe official NBA rules to ensure fair play and guard against injury, and the referees are there to make sure the rules are followed to the letter. When a ref spots a foul, he or she blows a whistle to stop play. Depending on the foul, a referee can award the other team possession of the ball or free throws. (Any player who is called for six fouls in a game must leave and cannot return to that game.) Referees have to know the game's rules thoroughly to perform their job in a loud, pressure-packed arena. Refs make their decisions in a split second, so they rely on experience and training to help them make the right call.

KNOW THE SCORE
Official scorers, who sit courtside and assist the referees, use a book like this one to keep careful count of all the statistics during a game and a season.

Zipper

BLACK-AND-WHITE STRIPES
Referees are sometimes called "zebras" after the black-and-white shirts they wore for a time, such as this one worn by Pat Kennedy during the 1949–50 season. Today's officials wear the gray, short-sleeved, V-necked shirts shown at right.

Old NBA logo

PAT KENNEDY
Hall of Famer Pat Kennedy was a showman on the court, known for making his calls with animated gestures. Here, Kennedy wears an old-fashioned long-sleeved official's uniform.

Blue stripes denote an NBA official.

Signal for "grabbing wrist" foul

Slot official watches players away from the ball.

INSTANT REPLAY
NBA and WNBA referees use courtside monitors to view taped replays of game action and double-check close calls. For instance, since shots taken at the end of a period only count if the shot is in the air when the period-ending buzzer sounds, a ref must check to see whether a shot was released on time. Refs can also check the position of a player's feet to verify a three-point shot.

Trail official covers the ball behind the free-throw line.

Lead official covers the ball from basket to free-throw line.

player movement	● referee
defense	□ defense
referee movement	○ offense

FULL-COURT COVERAGE
Three officials are located on the court at all times. Each official covers a certain section of the court to ensure that no violations are missed; the referees rotate around the action as a play develops. The NBA added the third referee prior to the 1988–89 season. Before then, the league used two officials per game.

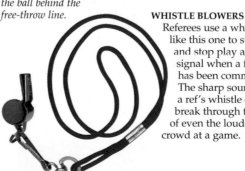

WHISTLE BLOWERS
Referees use a whistle like this one to start and stop play and to signal when a foul has been committed. The sharp sound of a ref's whistle can break through the din of even the loudest crowd at a game.

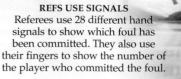

REFS USE SIGNALS
Referees use 28 different hand signals to show which foul has been committed. They also use their fingers to show the number of the player who committed the foul.

The referee signals that number 53 has fouled. (The left hand shows the five and the right hand the three.)

COMMUNICATION
Referees and players sometimes don't see eye to eye. Players and officials often talk during a game about a call the official has made. Being able to communicate clearly with players is an important skill for officials.

WNBA logo

Red stripes denote a WNBA official.

FEMALE REFS
The WNBA has featured female referees since the league started in 1997. That year, women were also hired to officiate men's games, making the NBA the first professional men's league to hire women referees.

Referees use this device to restart the clock after breaks.

EVERYBODY KNOWS EARL
Earl Strom was one of the NBA's greatest and most recognizable referees. He officiated in the league for 29 years and called 295 NBA playoff games, including 29 NBA Finals. He also worked in seven All-Star Games and was inducted into the Basketball Hall of Fame in 1995.

Footwear

NBA PLAYERS RUN AS MUCH AS FOUR MILES during a game, so what they wear on their feet is almost as important as how they shoot their jump shots. Today's basketball shoes have come a long way from the canvas-and-rubber models of earlier days. Today, technology plays a big part in designing shoes and developing materials to make shoes that can withstand the pounding dished out by players. The great performance—and fancy styling—of sneakers worn by NBA players has also made them popular with fans.

UNDERNEATH THE SHOES
As early as 1910 and into the 1950s, players wore cotton stockings called stirrups (left) that resembled gear worn by baseball players. An elastic band at the top helped keep them from falling down. Today's players wear a variety of styles of socks, often in team colors and featuring the NBA logo (right). Most players today wear very short socks, rather than the knee-length socks popular into the 1980s.

Stirrup wrapped under a player's foot.

Feet firsts

The first basketball shoes were made by Spalding Sporting Goods in 1903. The shoes featured "suction sole" bottoms for better stability and grip on wood floors. Some very early shoes were made of canvas and were low cut, but high-top shoes became the standard by around 1910.

Canvas uppers

Leather uppers

Converse All Star, 1930s

Thick rubber sole

JAMES JUMPS
Many NBA players endorse particular brands of shoes, wearing them in games or helping create their own customized models. LeBron James of the Cleveland Cavaliers often wears these all-black shoes. James helped design them to help players run, jump, and move quickly and safely on the court.

CLASSIC "CHUCKS"
The Converse All Star is the best selling basketball shoe of all time. The canvas shoes, first made in 1917, were later named for Chuck Taylor, the player who inspired their creation.

Converse logo

Thick red laces give a hint of the vivid designs to come.

Leather shoe, early 1900s

Taylor's signature

Converse All Star, 1960s

Holes for laces

Foam inner
padding

INSIDE THE SHOE
This NBA shoe by Reebok is made of 14
different materials, all designed with weight
and durability in mind. Basketball shoes
need to be able to put up with heavy action,
but also be light enough to let players move
easily in them. It takes over two hours to
assemble just one of these high-tech shoes.

Reinforced back to protect heel

*Lining made of
lightweight material
called Tricot, designed
to absorb moisture*

Foam padding

Padded tongue

*Air pocket
for added
flexibility*

*Thicker rubber
in the heel*

Computer-designed
treads

High-abrasion rubber

Air-filled plastic insert

TRACTION ACTION
Besides comfort, the most important aspect of a basketball shoe is
traction—how the sneaker helps the player move safely on the court.
Players need shoes that grip the floor to help them make sharp cuts
and quick turns. This shoe features a herringbone tread pattern
designed especially for use on a basketball court.

REVOLUTIONARY SHOES
As a player, Michael Jordan had an
enormous impact on the sport. His
namesake Nike "Air Jordan" shoes
had just as big an impact on the
fashion world. Introduced in 1984,
they were among the
first basketball shoes
to use color in
their design.

Finger loop

Nylon-covered padding

Ventilation
holes

Holes for laces

FANCY FOOTWEAR
Style, comfort, technology, and performance all come together
in shoes worn by NBA players. The NBA "Denial" shoe by
Reebok rises to a player's ankle, higher than old-time
low-tops, but shorter than classic Chuck Taylors and
other high-tops. The bright blue padding on the
top is for both style and support, while the
lightweight plastic insert in the heel
helps comfort the foot.

Leather upper

Air pocket

Solid
arch
supports feet.

*Colored panels
made of synthetic
material*

Uniforms and gear

UNLIKE PLAYERS IN MANY OTHER SPORTS, basketball players need very little clothing or gear in their game. Players wear sleeveless shirts and shorts, along with shoes and socks. The first uniforms were very plain, heavy wool shirts, which soon gave way to more comfortable cotton tank tops. As teams and leagues began to develop, identifying logos and numbers were added. Polyester was introduced after World War II, then a nylon mesh was used to keep players even cooler. Today's uniforms are made of high-tech performance material, but the look is much the same as the earliest basketball gear.

Sleeves could be folded back for ease of movement.

The class of 1915 wore this uniform.

Puffy bloomer suits reached well below the knees.

Warm-up clothing

During pregame practice or on the sidelines, players wear warm-up clothing over their uniforms. The original warm-ups were made of wool and later nylon, and consisted of thick pants and a jacket. Today's warm-up gear is made of lightweight synthetic fabric designed to help control body temperature and keep players dry.

FASHION AND FUNCTION
Warm-up suits are not just for looks—they can help a player's performance by keeping muscles warm and limber. Here, LeBron James and Richard Hamilton relax before a game in official warm-up gear.

COVER ALL
The first women's uniforms, such as this example from a college team of 1915, were called "bloomer suits." Designed in a modest time to cover the entire body, they came with stockings that covered the lower legs.

1943 WARM-UPS
This uniquely styled Zollner Pistons warm-up suit was made of wool and nylon. Most college and pro teams of the day featured snaps or zippers on the jackets.

Pull-away snaps

Warm lining

Cotton terry material

Miami Heat logo

SWEATBANDS
Terry-cloth head- and wristbands first appeared in the late 1960s to keep sweat away from players' eyes and hands.

Elastic waistband

Team color

NBA logo

EASY OFF
Featuring team colors, a warm lining, and pull-away snaps, today's NBA warm-up pants are among the most fashionable pieces of basketball gear. To help players get onto the court quickly during play, the pants snap all the way down. Instead of pulling the pants off over their shoes, players simply pull the two sides apart and step away.

Miami Heat logo

Uniforms

Though short- or long-sleeved shirts were common in the 1890s, tank top jerseys came to stay in the early 1900s. Still, uniforms have evolved over time, changing materials, colors, and lengths year by year.

Mikan was voted the "Greatest Player in the First Half-Century" by The Associated Press.

Cotton jersey

Polyester

Sewn-on uniform numbers

Attached belt

Buttons to keep uniform in place

Button-crotch college jersey, 1950s

George Mikan, Minneapolis Lakers, 1950s

Protective gear

Unfortunately, players can get hurt during games. To help prevent injuries, protective gear is available for almost every part of the body—from eye goggles and face masks to elbow and knee pads. Early equipment may look rough, but many players welcomed the added protection.

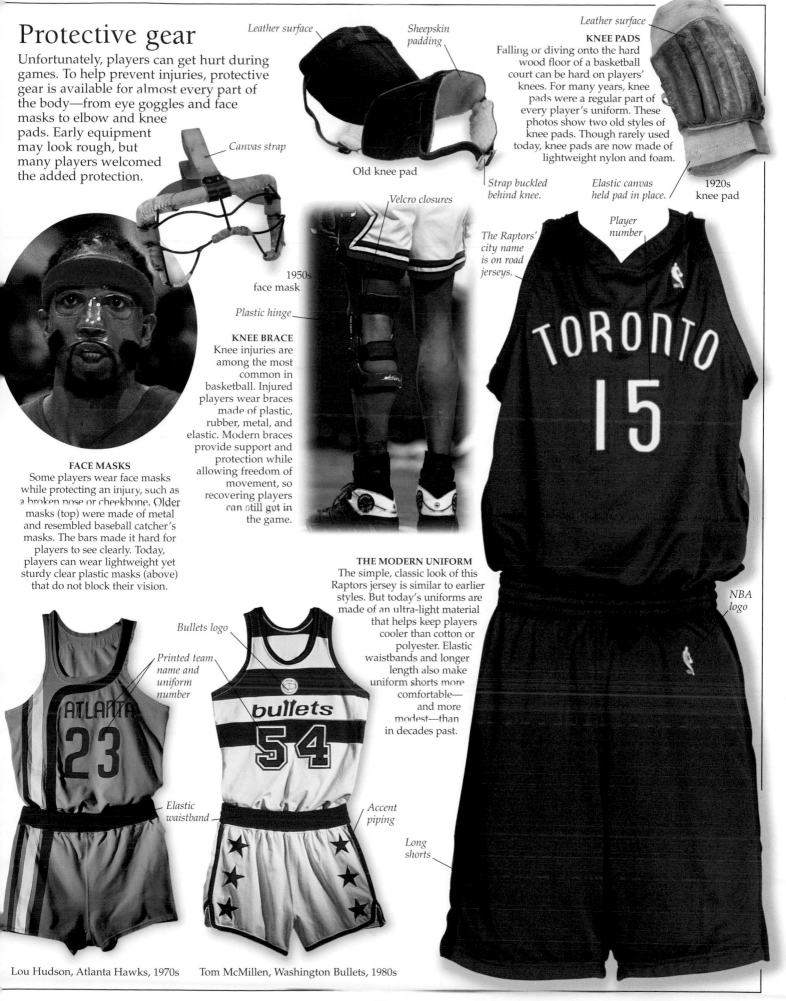

Leather surface

Sheepskin padding

Old knee pad

Canvas strap

KNEE PADS
Falling or diving onto the hard wood floor of a basketball court can be hard on players' knees. For many years, knee pads were a regular part of every player's uniform. These photos show two old styles of knee pads. Though rarely used today, knee pads are now made of lightweight nylon and foam.

Leather surface

Strap buckled behind knee.

Elastic canvas held pad in place.

1920s knee pad

Velcro closures

1950s face mask

Plastic hinge

KNEE BRACE
Knee injuries are among the most common in basketball. Injured players wear braces made of plastic, rubber, metal, and elastic. Modern braces provide support and protection while allowing freedom of movement, so recovering players can still get in the game.

FACE MASKS
Some players wear face masks while protecting an injury, such as a broken nose or cheekbone. Older masks (top) were made of metal and resembled baseball catcher's masks. The bars made it hard for players to see clearly. Today, players can wear lightweight yet sturdy clear plastic masks (above) that do not block their vision.

Player number

The Raptors' city name is on road jerseys.

THE MODERN UNIFORM
The simple, classic look of this Raptors jersey is similar to earlier styles. But today's uniforms are made of an ultra-light material that helps keep players cooler than cotton or polyester. Elastic waistbands and longer length also make uniform shorts more comfortable— and more modest—than in decades past.

NBA logo

Bullets logo

Printed team name and uniform number

Elastic waistband

Accent piping

Long shorts

Lou Hudson, Atlanta Hawks, 1970s   Tom McMillen, Washington Bullets, 1980s

Shooting

SHOOTING IS BASKETBALL'S MOST basic move. Players try to sink the ball in the basket, scoring points for their team when it goes through. There are many forms of shooting: jump shots, hook shots, lay ups, free throws, banks shots, and more. In a game situation, players choose one shot or another depending on the scoring opportunity.

A GAME SAVER
The 24-second shot clock, introduced in 1954, helped increase scoring in the NBA. After getting the ball, teams must get off a shot that at least hits the rim within this time.

Shooters always keep their eyes on the basket.

THREE-POINT SPECIALISTS
The three-point line made its NBA debut in the 1979–80 season. A shot made from behind a line (about 23 feet from the basket) is worth three points, one more than a normal basket. It is a valuable offensive option, especially to sharp-shooting players such as Peja Stojakovic (16).

Stojakovic jumps to get a clear shot.

Lay ups are usually released with one hand.

NBA SCORING KING
On April 5, 1984, Kareem Abdul-Jabbar used this ball to pass NBA legend Wilt Chamberlain and become the NBA's all-time scoring leader. The six-time NBA champion retired five seasons later, finishing his career with an NBA-record 38,387 points.

Players approach the basket from one side or the other for a lay up.

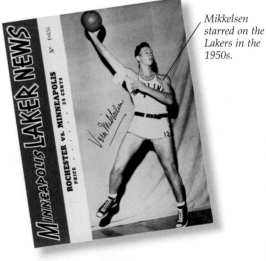

Mikkelsen starred on the Lakers in the 1950s.

LAY UP
The lay up is the most common way to score in basketball. An easy shot from close to the basket, a lay up can be made with or without using the backboard. Lay ups often result after a player drives to the basket or finishes a fast break. As his teammate "boxes out" the opponent (see Glossary), Brad Miller of the Sacramento Kings jumps toward the basket and softly bounces the ball off the backboard and into the net.

HOOK SHOT
The hook shot is one of the most effective shooting styles. Vern Mikkelsen of the Minneapolis Lakers demonstrates the move on this program cover, reaching high above his head to throw with one hand.

HALF-COURT SHOT
Sinking a half-court shot requires skill, strength, and luck. This fan tests his long-range skills in a contest held during a break in a game.

HIT AND MISS
Shot charts keep track of whether shots are made or missed. This helps determine the success rate of a player or a team. Opponents also chart shots to aid the defense.

○	missed
●	scored

Free throw shooting

On some fouls, players are awarded a free throw from a line 15 feet from the basket. A successful shot is worth one point. Though they look simple, free throws require concentration, form, and proper follow-through, often under intense pressure. Many games are won or lost at the free throw line.

Miller steadies the ball with both hands before releasing it with his right.

Mike Dunleavy releases the ball with one hand.

CHARITY STRIPE
Since foul shots are undefended, some players refer to the free-throw line as a "charity stripe." But a successful shot takes work: Players spend hours of practice refining their technique.

ONE-HANDED SHOT
Most players shoot free throws in a similar style. They square their shoulders and feet to the basket, set themselves, and try to use a single, smooth motion to push the ball toward the goal. Some players also dribble the ball before shooting to help get their rhythm.

Barry used his thumbs to create backspin on his free throws.

UNDERHAND THROW
The underhand style of free-throw shooting isn't common, but it's certainly effective. Hall of Famer Rick Barry used this style to rack up the second highest free-throw percentage in NBA history (.900). He made 3,818 of his 4,243 attempts.

Bent knees add stability.

CLASSIC JUMP SHOT
The jump shot was first used in basketball in the 1920s. It didn't take hold in the NBA until the late 1940s, and even then the set shot (in which a player's feet stayed on the ground) was more common. In a jump shot, the player shoots the ball at the basket from over his head while at the very top of a straight upward leap. Throughout the decades, many great shooters have refined the art of the jump shot. Reggie Miller (right) is one of those players; he has used this classic form to become one of the NBA's greatest clutch jump shooters.

The shot is taken when the feet reach the top of the jump.

Ballhandling

BEFORE EVEN TAKING A SHOT, players use a variety of skills to move the ball around the court and into scoring position. The rules of basketball require the ball to be in motion almost all the time, so dribbling—or bouncing—and passing the ball are critical. Dribbling allows a player to move with the ball, whether running down the court or taking a layup at the net. Basic passes between players help move the ball quickly through opponents. To prepare for the fast pace and defensive pressure of game time, top players practice these skills for hours on end.

IN A SPIN
Chris Webber shows off a favorite ball-handling trick: spinning the ball on one finger.

Thumbs turn inward as ball is released.

Fingers push the ball forward.

CHEST PASS
This the most common type of pass. With both hands on the ball, the player pushes firmly outward with his hands and arms, directing the ball to a teammate.

TRANSITION PASSING
Moving the ball quickly up court after a missed shot starts with the transition pass. A defender (left) jumps to grab the ball off the backboard, then passes it to a teammate (right) even before landing from his jump. His teammate then dribbles the ball up the court toward the goal. This quick movement can lead to a fast break (a rush up court by the offense), or other scoring opportunities.

Andre Miller grabs the pass before running the ball up court.

Knees are bent, ready to run.

Josh Childress adds power by stepping one foot in the direction of the pass.

Damon Stoudamire shows how to confuse defenders by looking one way as the pass goes another.

Elton Brand's feet are still in the air after a rebound.

Players practice dribbling without watching the ball, as Latrell Sprewell demonstrates.

A snap of the wrist makes passes more crisp.

BOUNCE PASS
Like a chest pass, the bounce pass is released from above the waist. The ball is bounced off the floor to a teammate, so this low pass is good for avoiding the outstretched arms of defenders.

DRIBBLE DRIVE
Shielding the ball with one side, a player dribbles with his other hand while running toward the basket. Good dribblers can cut through and around defenders. Players are not allowed to run with the ball without dribbling, so this skill is worth practicing to be able to move quickly and keep defenders on their toes.

DRILL, DRILL, DRILL
The best players know that constant practice is what makes a player ready for a game. With the fundamentals learned by heart and drilled at every practice, players in a game situation can respond to specific obstacles quickly and creatively—without worrying about the basics.

Mike Bibby of the Sacramento Kings works on his ball-control skills in a practice game.

Pebbled texture

Rubber seam

Vince Carter "palms" the ball.

PALMING THE BALL
Some players' hands are large enough to palm (hold with one hand) a basketball—or even two. For all players, the slightly bumpy leather surface of the ball helps improve grip.

WRAPAROUND PASS
One way of attacking a larger opponent is to pass around him. A smaller player (Sam Casell, in blue) draws a larger defender (Brad Miller) and then passes around that player to an open teammate. Iverson's teammate, of course, must be aware of his plan and move to an open spot, otherwise he might find himself in mid air with no one to pass to. Like all the passes shown on this page, it takes two players working together to be effective.

"HOUDINI OF THE HARDWOOD"
Bob Cousy is shown here in a multiple-exposure photo demonstrating the ball-handling skills that earned him that nickname (after the famous magician). The Boston Celtics Hall of Famer popularized crowd-pleasing plays such as dribbling between the legs or passing behind the back.

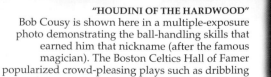

Defense

WHILE TOP SCORERS GET MOST OF THE GLORY, basketball insiders know that defense is often just as big a part of the story of a successful team. After all, a team will spend about half of each game trying to stop its opponent from scoring. Players must use quickness, good defensive techniques, and solid team strategies to prevent opponents from getting off good shots, or to keep them from penetrating close to the basket. The best defenders can anticipate an opponent's next move and be in the right position to stop it.

BILL RUSSELL: A DEFENSIVE FORCE
Bill Russell (6) was a star center for the Boston Celtics in the 1950s and 1960s. He was one of the few players who could dominate the game without scoring a lot of points—simply by playing great defense. Russell excelled at blocking shots (as he shows here), often turning them into fast breaks for his team.

Players can grab rebounds with one hand, as Eduardo Najera does here, or with both hands.

NBA Defensive Player of the Year Trophy

Mark Blount tries to distract the shooter with his hand.

TOP DEFENDER
The NBA Defensive Player of the Year award is given annually to the player who most excels at skills such as rebounding and blocking shots. Detroit Pistons center Ben Wallace is a two-time winner of the award.

Defender Paul Pierce squares himself between his opponent and the basket.

GUARDING A SHOOTER
Players can try to disrupt an opponent who is shooting by jumping in front of him and raising a hand or arm. They are not allowed to make contact with the shooter, however.

Manu Ginobili tries to make a play for the offense.

CLEANING THE GLASS
When a shot does not go in the basket, either team can "rebound," or recover the ball. Defensive rebounding is essential, as this prevents an opponent from getting off another quick shot. The "glass" is a nickname for the backboard. A rebound is also commonly referred to as a "board."

PRESSURE DEFENSE
Pressure defense, or "playing tight," is a common defensive tactic. It's often used against smaller players who rely more on ball-handling than on body mass. Defenders try to pressure their opponents into making a mistake and losing control of the ball. Defenders cannot grab or push an opponent while guarding him.

REJECTION!

That is what announcers and fans say when a defender blocks an opponent's shot, as Kobe Bryant (in white) does here. Along with stopping potential goals, a player who can block shots is a very intimidating force near the basket, often forcing opponents to change their plan of attack to avoid him. Note that shots can only be blocked on their way up from a player's hand; once the ball is on its way down to the basket, a shot can't be blocked. If it is, the referee will call a foul called goaltending and award the shooter the points for his shot.

Bryant tries to touch only the ball, not the shooter.

ZONE DEFENSE

The 1-2-2 zone defense shown here is illegal in the NBA, but is used often in college ball. In a zone, one player stands at the top of the lane, and two pairs of two players stay nearer the basket. Rather than guarding a specific player, defenders in a zone are responsible for guarding an area of the court.

Defenders in a zone stay close to the free-throw lane.

MAN-TO-MAN DEFENSE

The most common defense used is called man-to-man. Each defender is assigned a specific opponent and must follow that player wherever he goes. Teammates must be ready to switch players quickly if they are blocked from their assigned opponent. Defenders must also know where the ball is at all times.

Defenders run wherever their opponents run.

FULL COURT PRESS

After a team scores, the opposing team throws the ball in-bounds to restart play, then runs it toward their goal. Instead of waiting for the offense to bring the ball down court to start playing defense, some teams use this full court press. The defense puts extra pressure on the player with the ball as soon as it is passed in-bounds. The goal is to use pressure to create mistakes. It is often used against slower teams or late in games.

Team A tries to regain possession and return the ball to their basket at the other end of the court.

KEY:

5	Team A
5	Team B
→	player moves
⇢	ball moves

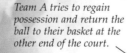

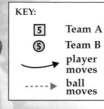

23

Slam Dunk

SOME CONSIDER THE SLAM DUNK THE MOST exciting play in basketball. While most shots are taken from some distance away from the basket—ranging from a few feet to the long-distance three-point shot—the dunk is right up close. To make a dunk, players leap high above their opponents. With one hand or two, they slam the ball into the hoop, often after passing the ball from hand to hand, pumping it up and down, or spinning their bodies. The first slam-dunk artist was Lakers forward Elgin Baylor in the late 1950s and 1960s. Others have followed, including Connie Hawkins, Julius "Dr. J." Erving, Michael Jordan, and Vince Carter. Since 1984, the annual Slam Dunk Contest has crowned the game's mid-air master.

Net made of nylon cording

Metal arm

RIM ON A SPRING
In the early days of dunking, powerful players occasionally ripped the metal rims out of the backboards. Modern baskets feature a rim that is attached with a strong spring that gives slightly, protecting both the player and the basket.

SPUD SOARS TO DUNKING LORE
The game's top dunkers gather to show their skills at the annual Slam Dunk Contest, held the day before the All-Star Game. In 1986, 5' 7" Spud Webb of the Atlanta Hawks put on one of the greatest shows in contest history—including an amazing slam that netted a perfect score of 50. Holding the ball with two hands, Spud leaped, held the ball between his legs, then spun his body completely around before ramming the ball into the basket.

Most dunkers hold the ball with one hand.

1986 NBA Slam Dunk Contest trophy

Webb's feet were nearly four feet from the floor on this dunk.

MICHAEL JORDAN: AERIAL MASTER
Michael Jordan is considered by many as the greatest player in NBA history. The 6' 6" shooting guard dominated his competition with all-around athleticism rooted in basketball fundamentals. But it was his stunning success in the air that excited the fans. He seemed to defy gravity as he soared and scored with awesome dunks. Jordan won the 1987 and 1988 NBA Slam Dunk contests. Today, a statue of Michael Jordan (in flight) is featured in front of Chicago's United Center arena.

In the classic slam dunk, the player's hand literally "stuffs," or slams, the ball through the rim.

DUNKING PRODIGY
The Lakers' Kobe Bryant was only 18 when he won the 1997 NBA Slam Dunk Contest. He continues to thrill fans during games, soaring above opponents as he does here. Like Vince Carter, Michael Jordan, and other slam-dunk stars, Bryant makes this move only one of many talents in his arsenal. The height and power behind this dunk show why it can be an almost unblockable part of a team's offensive attack.

Wristband to help keep hands dry

THE DOCTOR IS IN
Julius Erving demonstrates classic slam dunk form. Erving, known as "Dr. J.," was one of the players most responsible for spreading the popularity of the slam dunk, and one of the most creative dunkers in NBA history.

SIR CHARLES
Charles Barkley starred on several teams with a combination of athleticism, power, and sheer force. His dunks were usually more a product of strength and power than grace and style.

Carter brings the ball between his legs before grabbing it with his right hand to slam it home.

TORONTO'S SKYWALKER
The art of dunking reached a new level in 2000 when Vince Carter won the NBA Slam Dunk Contest in Oakland. The 6' 6" All-Star unveiled an assortment of gravity-defying dunks, including a between-the-legs aerial special that earned a perfect score of 50 from the judges. Carter, like other dunking artists, often showcases his specialty in games as well as the contests.

Strategy

A BASKETBALL GAME CAN SOMETIMES APPEAR to be very disorganized, with players running back and forth over and over. In reality, many of a team's movements on the court are carefully planned by the team's coaches. Along with an overall plan of attack, a team can also use some of the basic plays diagrammed on these pages. Of course, while a team tries to use a planned strategy, sometimes a game dictates that a creative player just make up a play as he goes!

BY THE NUMBERS
Coach Pat Riley diagrams a play using now-standard position numbers: 1: point guard; 2: shooting guard; 3: power forward; 4: small forward; 5: center.

Yao's practice shirt bears his uniform number.

Dry-erase surface for easy changes

WORKING ON STRATEGY AT PRACTICE
Players and coaches discuss strategy every day. To help them visualize new ideas, plays are sketched on an erasable white board like this one. This allows players and the coach to carefully go over how the players will move on the court before putting new moves into practice, and review practice or game scenarios after the fact.

Pre-printed court diagrams

GAME TIME
During timeouts like this one and at halftime, a coach talks with players about how the game is going, what the opponent is doing, and how the team needs to react. Here, the Spurs' Gregg Popovich talks with Tim Duncan. Popovich is one of only 12 coaches in NBA history to win two or more NBA titles.

Popovich uses a small, portable whiteboard to discuss plays during a game.

Future stars

Fayetteville Patriots jersey

Some players work on their skills and their knowledge of basketball plays and strategy by taking part in the National Basketball Development League (NBDL), which helps them improve before advancing to the NBA.

The NBDL uses the Spalding Infusion ball, which features a built-in air pump.

NBDL COACHING
The NBDL allows coaches such as Joey Meyer (above) to refine their basketball strategy skills and learn to work with young players.

Dwyane Wade on a lay-up

Tim Duncan sets the pick.

The defender is blocked by Duncan.

Tony Parker dribbles (or "rolls") around the pick.

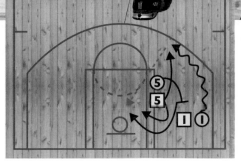

BACK DOOR PASS

This is a classic bit of basketball teamwork. In the diagram, green #3 passes to green #1. The passer then fakes a run to the corner and cuts quickly behind the defender (yellow #3) toward the basket. Green #1 then passes the ball back to his teammate, who grabs the ball and heads for the basket, often getting an easy lay up (left) as a reward for his work.

PICK AND ROLL

Like the back door pass, the pick and roll is a traditional way for teammates to work together to create scoring opportunities. In the diagram, green #1 leads his defender (yellow #1) toward green #5. Green #5 then blocks the defender, which is called "setting a pick." Green #1 can then dribble unguarded around the pick toward open space, freeing himself for a clean shot at the basket.

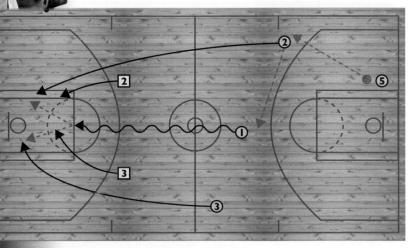

FAST BREAK

Fast breaks occur after a team misses a shot or a free throw. The rebounder (#5 in diagram) quickly passes to a teammate running up court (#1 in diagram; #24 in photo), who then dribbles quickly toward his team's basket for a pass or a shot.

The birth of the NBA

IN THE 1940s, MOST ARENAS IN THE UNITED STATES were used exclusively for hockey. But with college basketball surging in popularity and open dates on event calendars, arena owners in major cities such as Boston and New York began to think of filling empty seats with a men's pro basketball league. On June 6, 1946, the Basketball Association of America (BAA) was formed. A newer rival, the National Basketball League (NBL), featured star players such as George Mikan, but played in smaller markets and arenas. Slowly, NBL teams were absorbed by the BAA. After the 1948–49 season, the NBL disappeared as a league, and the BAA changed its name to the National Basketball Association. The NBA was born, with the league recognizing its first season as 1948–49.

THE FIRST GAME
Toronto was the site of the BAA's inaugural game, featuring the New York Knickerbockers and the Toronto Huskies. A crowd of 7,090 turned out at Maple Leaf Gardens on November 1, 1946, as the Knicks defeated the Huskies 68-66.

Wool jersey

Team owner's name

ZOLLNER PISTONS
Fred Zollner, the owner of a piston-manufacturing plant in Fort Wayne, Indiana, also owned a basketball team in the NBL called the Fort Wayne Zollner Pistons. (The team later moved to Detroit.) The Pistons' uniform featured the name of its owner on the heavy wool jersey, and a belt attached to the shorts to hold them up.

Howie Dallmar went on to coach Stanford University from 1955 to 1975.

THE 1946–47 NBA CHAMPION PHILADELPHIA WARRIORS
The Philadelphia Warriors defeated the Chicago Stags 4–1 in the 1947 NBA Finals to claim the league's first title. Joe Fulks (No. 10), Howie Dallmar (No. 12), and Angelo Musi (No. 5) starred in that series versus Chicago.

BAA logo

BEFORE THEY WERE KINGS
This patch adorned the uniforms of the Rochester Royals, who began play in 1948–49 as a member of the BAA, the forerunner to the NBA. The Royals reigned supreme in only their fourth season, defeating the New York Knicks 4–1 in the NBA Finals. The franchise relocated to Cincinnati before becoming the Kansas City/Omaha Kings in 1972. The Kings now play in Sacramento.

SYRACUSE'S FAVORITE SON
Dolph Schayes of the Syracuse Nationals was one of the NBA's greatest players, averaging 18.2 points per game during his 16-year career. The 12-time NBA All-Star also led the Nationals to the 1955 NBA title.

Fulks played for the Philadelphia Warriors from 1946 to 1954.

JUMPIN' JOE FULKS
Joe Fulks was the NBA's first great scorer, winning the league's scoring title in the 1946–47 season. Fulks was also one of the first great shooters, once scoring 63 points in a game— the eighth highest single-game scoring total in NBA history.

AFRICAN-AMERICAN PIONEER
Earl Lloyd (above), along with Nat "Sweetwater" Clifton and Chuck Cooper, were the first African-American players to play in the NBA. Lloyd logged the first minutes of action when he made his debut for the Washington Capitols on October 31, 1950.

Celtics owner Walter Brown

STAGS COME FIRST
Before the Chicago Bulls rose to the top of the NBA, the home team in this big city was the Stags. This ticket is from a 1949 game at the old Chicago Stadium.

"Talent" means players, who were given some tickets for friends and family.

THE MIGHTY BOSTON CELTICS
Head coach Red Auerbach (center) and the Boston Celtics celebrate the 1957 NBA title after defeating the St. Louis Hawks in a grueling, seven-game series. It was the first of many championships for the NBA's most successful franchise as Auerbach eventually presided over the greatest championship run in NBA history. Boston won eight consecutive titles from 1959 to 1966.

Basketball's first superstar

George Mikan, the 6' 10" center of the Minneapolis Lakers, was the NBA's first superstar. Mikan's success prompted a rules change to widen the lane beneath the basket (on offense, players can remain in the lane beneath the basket for only three seconds; a wider lane kept Mikan farther from the hoop), but the new rule didn't slow him down.

Dolph Schayes

MIKAN: QUITE A SPECTACLE
Mikan needed glasses to correct his vision, so his wire rim eye glasses were an important part of the center's game. This form of protective eye wear eventually gave way to plastic goggles in later years.

Adjustable leather strap

Mikan's eyeglasses

Wire rims

TROPHY PLAYER
In his nine-year career, George Mikan earned many individual awards in addition to the championships his teams won. Mikan received this trophy when he was named *Sport Magazine*'s 1949 Performer of the Year.

READ ALL ABOUT IT
Fans were able to follow their favorite teams by purchasing sports magazines and game programs, which provided profiles and statistics of their favorite players. The *Syracuse Sports Magazine* features the hometown Nationals, the only major league sports team in the city's history.

The 1960s

WILT'S 100
Wilt Chamberlain did the unthinkable when he became the only player ever to score 100 points in a single game. He did it on March 2, 1962, in Hershey, Pennsylvania.

IT WAS AN UNBELIEVABLE RUN, especially by today's standards: eight consecutive NBA championships (1959–1966) and 11 NBA titles in 13 seasons (1957–1969). Even beyond those stunning streaks by the Boston Celtics, what a decade it was for the NBA. Not only did Boston outplay all of its opponents, but the league experienced enormous growth as well. The NBA expanded to California in 1960, when the Lakers moved from Minneapolis to Los Angeles. The eight-team league that once didn't have a West Coast presence now featured teams in Phoenix, San Diego, San Francisco, and Seattle. The Sixties saw some of the NBA's greatest players flourish—Wilt Chamberlain, Oscar Robertson, Jerry West —but was dominated by one franchise: the Boston Celtics.

Johnny Most's famous radio call headlined a record album about the Celtics.

Robertson displays classic jump shooting form.

"HAVLICEK STOLE THE BALL!"
Johnny Most, the Boston Celtics' legendary broadcaster, shouted these words after John Havlicek deflected this Philadelphia 76ers inbounds pass—securing Boston's Game 7 victory in the 1965 Eastern Division Finals.

TRIPLE THREAT
One of the NBA's best all-around players, Oscar "The Big O" Robertson (14) is the only player to post a "triple double" (double-digit averages in three statistical categories) for an entire season. In 1961–62, he averaged 30.8 points, 11.4 assists, and 12.5 rebounds per game.

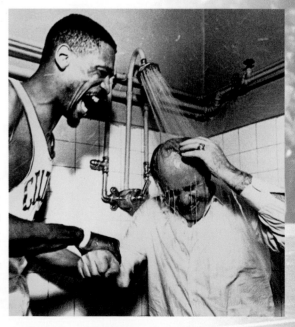

CELTICS DYNASTY
Center Bill Russell and coach Red Auerbach were the anchors of the greatest dynasty in NBA history. In the Celtics' amazing streak, Auerbach coached nine winners and was general manager for all 11. In 1966, Russell became the NBA's first African-American head coach.

RUSSELL VS. CHAMBERLAIN

Bill Russell and Wilt Chamberlain formed the greatest individual rivalry in NBA history. The two Hall of Famers matched up 142 times in 10 years with Russell's Celtics winning 85 of those games. It was a classic confrontation between the NBA's greatest defensive force, Russell, versus the league's most dominant offensive force, Chamberlain.

Russell blocks the shot.

Chamberlain attempts a lay up.

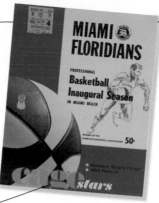

MIAMI FLORIDIANS

PROFESSIONAL

Basketball

Inaugural Season

IN MIAMI BEACH

50¢

★ ★

stars

A RIVAL LEAGUE

This game program is from the first season of the Miami Floridians in 1968. The team, originally from Minnesota, was one of the members of the brand-new American Basketball Association, founded to challenge the established NBA. The league started slowly in the late 1960s, but began to flourish in the 1970s.

Though the cages were long gone, the nickname for the game stuck.

Philadelphia's 76ers are named for that city's patriotic past; the Declaration of Independence was signed there in 1776.

ELGIN BAYLOR: THE ORIGINAL HIGH FLYER

The godfather of the high flyers in the NBA is Elgin Baylor. The 6' 5" forward is remembered as one of the first great dunkers. Baylor was also one of the NBA's most prolific scorers, accumulating more than 23,000 career points. He owns the NBA Finals single-game record for most points with 61.

JERRY WEST: MR. CLUTCH

This classic Jerry West basketball card features one of the NBA's greatest guards and clutch players. West played his entire 14-year career for the Los Angeles Lakers, and is the franchise's all-time leading scorer with 25,192 points. West and the Lakers went to the NBA Finals seven times before winning in 1972.

Low-top sneakers were popular in the 1960s.

Bandage used as protective leg wrap

JERRY
WEST
guard
LOS ANGELES

The 1970s

UNLIKE THE CELTICS-DOMINATED 1960S, it seemed like everybody had a shot in the 1970s. Eight different teams were crowned champion during the 1970s, the most in any 10-year period in NBA history. Five teams—Milwaukee (1971), Golden State (1975), Portland (1977), Washington (1978), and Seattle (1979)—each won their first NBA championship ever. The 1970s began with 14 teams in two divisions, but the league grew to 20 teams and four divisions by the end of the decade. How competitive was this era in the NBA? Teams with the best regular-season record made it to the NBA Finals only six times, and no team won the title two years in a row.

This version of the NBA championship trophy was used until 1978.

COAST-TO-COAST RIVALRY
The New York Knicks and Los Angeles Lakers met in the NBA Finals three times in four years in the early 1970s. The Knicks won their first title in 1970, and the Lakers won their first in 1972. This program is from the 1973 Finals, in which New York defeated L.A. in five games.

THE CAPTAIN
Willis Reed played center for the New York Knicks and helped lead them to two NBA titles in four years (1970 and 1973). Reed, nicknamed "the Captain," was the first player in NBA history to win regular season, All-Star, and Finals MVP honors in the same season.

PLAYOFF FEVER
The Braves called Buffalo home for eight seasons (1970–1978) before moving west to become the San Diego Clippers. The Braves featured 1975 NBA MVP Bob McAdoo and head coach Jack Ramsay.

Bullets forward Mitch Kupchak

Center Jack Sikma moves into position for a rebound.

ENCORE PERFORMANCE
In 1978 and 1979, the Washington Bullets and Seattle SuperSonics met in the NBA Finals. The Bullets won the first match-up (above), while the SuperSonics won their first and only NBA title in 1979.

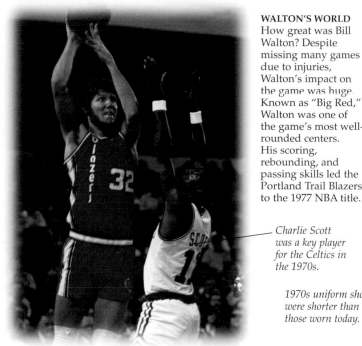

WALTON'S WORLD
How great was Bill Walton? Despite missing many games due to injuries, Walton's impact on the game was huge. Known as "Big Red," Walton was one of the game's most well-rounded centers. His scoring, rebounding, and passing skills led the Portland Trail Blazers to the 1977 NBA title.

Charlie Scott was a key player for the Celtics in the 1970s.

UPSET SPECIAL: WARRIORS WIN
"It has to be the greatest upset in the history of the NBA Finals," said Rick Barry. And he should know—Barry played a pivotal role in Golden State's upset of the heavily favored Washington Bullets in the 1975 NBA Finals. The Warriors shocked the basketball world by recording the first NBA Finals sweep in 29 years.

Wristband in team colors

1970s uniform shorts were shorter than those worn today.

EAST COAST RIVALRY
This ticket let a fan in to see a 1971 game featuring one of the NBA's fiercest rivalries, between the New York Knicks and the Baltimore Bullets.

Carvel logo

SWEET TREAT
Carvel Ice Cream Company honored Hall of Fame player Bill Bradley of the Knicks on this ice cream carton label. After retiring, Bradley became a U.S. Senator in 1979.

American Basketball Association (ABA)

The ABA tipped off on Feb. 1, 1967 and folded just nine years later, but its impact and spirit lives to this day. The league featured a red, white, and blue ball, three-point shooting, a dunk contest, and a wide-open, up-tempo, entertaining style of play. The league featured great players—Julius Erving, George Gervin, and David Thompson—who would later be NBA stars.

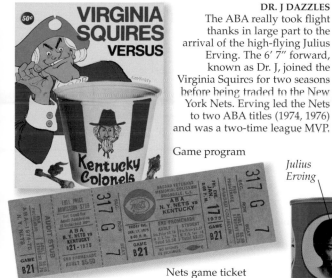

Game program

Nets game ticket

DR. J DAZZLES
The ABA really took flight thanks in large part to the arrival of the high-flying Julius Erving. The 6' 7" forward, known as Dr. J, joined the Virginia Squires for two seasons before being traded to the New York Nets. Erving led the Nets to two ABA titles (1974, 1976) and was a two-time league MVP.

Julius Erving

Soda can

NEW MARKETS
One of the most important things the ABA did for pro basketball was to bring the game to new cities. The Kentucky Colonels, Virginia Squires, and New Jersey Nets (program and ticket above) were among the teams that opened up these markets to the pro game. Virginia and Kentucky were already home to top college basketball programs.

PISTOL PETE
"Pistol" Pete Maravich was the ultimate basketball showman. A five-time All-Star, he led the NBA in scoring in 1977.

The 1980s

TWO STORIED FRANCHISES —the Los Angeles Lakers and the Boston Celtics— were once again the big story in the 1980s. The rival teams starred two players whose own rivalry would become one of the NBA's greatest stories: Multi-talented point guard Magic Johnson led the Lakers to five titles in the 1980s, while sharp-shooting Larry Bird helped the Celtics win three. Together, the duo helped the league reach new heights of popularity. 1984 was marked by the arrival of a rookie named Michael Jordan, who would take over where the Magic-Bird rivalry left off. During this decade, the NBA grew from 22 to 27 teams.

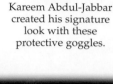

FAMOUS GOGGLES
Six-time NBA MVP Kareem Abdul-Jabbar created his signature look with these protective goggles.

THE HUMAN HIGHLIGHT FILM
Dominique Wilkins starred for the Atlanta Hawks in the 1980s. The nine-time All-Star and Hawks' all-time leading scorer earned his nickname for his wide array of high-flying dunks.

THE ONE AND ONLY DR. J
Julius "Dr. J" Erving was one of basketball's greatest leapers and dunkers. He led the 76ers to three NBA Finals appearances in the 1980s. They won the NBA title in 1983.

Clyde Drexler trading card

CLYDE THE GLIDE
Though only 6' 7", Clyde "The Glide" Drexler spent most of his time in the air as one of the game's greatest jumpers. He used his high-flying game to become the Portland Trail Blazers' all-time leading scorer.

D.C. MONUMENTS
Three-time NBA MVP Moses Malone (left) teamed with 7' 7" center Manute Bol (right) to create an imposing front line force on Washington Bullets teams starting in 1986. They're posing in front of their city's Washington Monument. In 1997, the Bullets changed their name to the Wizards.

MEDIA CREDENTIALS
These NBA Finals passes were given to media covering the 1986 NBA championship series. Print and broadcast journalists from around the world covered this and other Finals, using credentials (media passes) like these issued by the NBA. In 1986, they told the story of a great series, won by the Celtics in six games over the Houston Rockets.

FRENCH LICK INDIANA

Bird was nicknamed "the Hick from French Lick" after his tiny home town.

MAGIC AND BIRD

They began the rivalry in college, when Bird and Indiana State lost to Magic and Michigan State in the 1979 NCAA Finals. The competition continued in the NBA, where their teams met in the Finals three times in the 1980s (below). Both players displayed some of the greatest all-around skills in NBA history.

OFFICIAL 1980-81
NBA GUIDE

The league celebrated its 35th anniversary in 1981.

ANOTHER CELTICS STAR

Kevin McHale was one of the Boston Celtics' most valuable players in the eighties. He teamed with Larry Bird and Robert Parish to earn Boston three NBA titles. McHale's long arms made him difficult to guard near the basket. He was the first player in NBA history to make 60 percent of his shots from the field and 80 percent from the free-throw line in the same season.

Bird and Magic were featured on the league's official media guide for the 1980–81 season.

Celtics logo on center court at the Boston Garden

BOSTON 1986 WORLD CHAMPIONS CELTICS

1986 Celtics pennant

TITLE IN DETROIT

Isiah Thomas led the Detroit Pistons in the 1980s. The talented point guard used his passing and shooting skills to help the Pistons win the 1989 NBA title, which they would repeat the next year, too.

WORLD CHAMPS 1989

1989 Pistons pennant

The 1990s

WHEN THE 1990s began, star guard and scoring champion Michael Jordan of the Chicago Bulls was in search of his first NBA championship ring.

As the decade drew to a close, Jordan and the Bulls had six. As the Celtics dominated the sport in the 1960s, the Bulls commanded the 1990s. In 1993, their streak was interrupted when Jordan announced his retirement. The Houston Rockets, led by All-Star center Hakeem Olajuwon, took full advantage, winning two championship titles in a row. But when Jordan returned for good in the 1995–96 season, the Bulls picked up right where they left off, winning another three NBA titles in a row (1996, 1997, and 1998).

CHAMPIONSHIP EMBRACE
Michael Jordan achieved his ultimate goal in 1991, when he won his first NBA championship. The 1991 NBA Finals showcased Magic Johnson and the Los Angeles Lakers versus Jordan and the Bulls. The Bulls won the title in five games. Afterward, an emotional Jordan hugged the championship trophy.

HOUSTON'S CHAMPIONSHIP LAUNCH
Hakeem "The Dream" Olajuwon secured the Houston Rockets' place in NBA championship history. The 6' 10" center from Nigeria led the Rockets to back-to-back titles in 1994 and 1995. Olajuwon combined rock-solid defense with outstanding offensive skills like few other players of his time.

CHARLES IN CHARGE
After spending six seasons in Philadelphia, Charles Barkley changed teams. The outspoken and extremely talented power forward joined the Phoenix Suns in 1992. In his first season, Barkley led Phoenix to their first NBA Finals appearance in 17 years and earned NBA MVP honors.

Bullish Run

From 1991 to 1998, the Chicago Bulls enjoyed one of the greatest championship runs in NBA history, stampeding to six NBA titles. Only the Boston Celtics have won more championships in an eight-year period. The trio of Michael Jordan, Scottie Pippen, and head coach Phil Jackson were the constants during the Bulls' historic march.

The game clock shows 6.6 seconds left as Jordan's shot heads toward the basket.

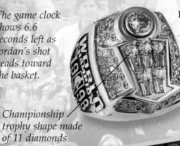

RING MASTERS
The Chicago Bulls' ring collection grew considerably in the 1990s. This 1998 diamond-filled edition is a 14-karat yellow gold ring that highlights the Bulls' six titles.

Championship trophy shape made of 11 diamonds

PENNANT FEVER: CHICAGO BULLS STYLE
The popularity of the Chicago Bulls continued to grow as the team won more titles—and fans loved cheering the champions. This pennant celebrates all six NBA titles claimed by Chicago in the 1990s.

JORDAN TO THE RESCUE—ONCE AGAIN

Michael Jordan's greatness was defined in part by his ability to come through in clutch moments. Jordan once again rose to the occasion in Game 6 of the 1998 NBA Finals. With only seconds remaining and the Bulls trailing by one, Jordan nailed this game-winning shot, giving Chicago the title.

Larry O'Brien NBA Championship Trophy

NBA Finals MVP Trophy

SPURRED TO SUCCESS
The San Antonio Spurs became the fourth NBA team in the 1990s to win an NBA championship. David Robinson and Tim Duncan led the way as the Spurs defeated the New York Knicks in five games in the 1999 NBA Finals. San Antonio became the first former ABA team to win an NBA title.

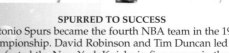

The NBA today

At 7' 1", Shaquille O'Neal is one of the NBA's biggest players.

WELCOME TO THE NBA— 21st century style! The league today is a far cry from the days of the first nine teams, when a western road trip went no farther than St. Louis and Minneapolis. The NBA today features 29 teams—with one more on the way in Charlotte—in two countries, and more than 400 players from around the world. The league is also on-line with NBA.com, so fans can follow their favorite players and teams no matter how far from an arena they are.

READ TO ACHIEVE
When they're not scoring on the court, NBA players such as Juwan Howard make a difference off the court. They take part in the NBA's Read to Achieve program, which promotes the value of reading and encourages adults to read regularly with children.

Pierce watches defenders as he dribbles.

Wearing a headband helps keep sweat out of a player's eyes.

LAKER LEGENDS
They are the highest-scoring and most successful duo in the NBA today. Shaquille O'Neal and Kobe Bryant led the Los Angeles Lakers to three consecutive NBA championships (2000–2002; see pennant at top) and have their eye on at least a few more before their jerseys are raised to the rafters to join the many other greats in the long history of the Lakers.

Official Spalding NBA ball

Pierce's sneakers are accented in Celtics green.

CELTIC PRIDE
How good is Paul Pierce? In the 2001–02 season, only his third in the NBA, the 6' 7" forward scored more than 2,000 points. The last Celtics great to do that was Larry Bird. Nicknamed "The Truth," Pierce is one of the NBA's premier players.

Size 22EEE shoes

Elastic elbow sleeve provides support and protection.

All NBA jerseys have the player's name and number on the back.

Modern NBA uniform shorts are much longer than their predecessors, reaching to the players' knees.

Elastic neoprene knee brace

Size 14 shoes

BRYANT 8

THE ANSWER
Don't let his relatively small size fool you—Allen Iverson of the Philadelphia 76ers is one tough player. At 6' 0" and 165 pounds, he is one of the smallest players in the NBA, but he is also one of the quickest. He has fought his way through bigger players under the basket to win three scoring titles and was named the league's MVP for the 2000–01 season.

Official NBA Encyclopedia

Hoop magazine

Desk calendar

Inside Stuff magazine

Video game

MULTIMEDIA BASKETBALL
Fans can learn more about their favorite teams and players by reading Hoop magazine, sold at newsstands and at arenas, and Inside Stuff, the league's teen publication. Video games are another way fans interact with their heroes.

All shapes and sizes

BASKETBALL IS NOT NECCESARILY A TALL PERSON'S game. Nor is it a game solely for big jumpers. The beauty of basketball is that it can be mastered by players of all shapes and sizes. Take Allen Iverson of the Philadelphia 76ers: He is barely six feet tall and weighs 165 pounds—petite by basketball standards—yet he is one of the league's toughest players, using his speed and agility to beat players who are a foot taller and weigh 100 pounds more than him. On the other end of the spectrum is Shaquille O'Neal, a 7' 1", 335-pound giant who is unstoppable under the basket because of his sheer size and strength.

DAVID VS. GOLIATH
At 5' 5", Earl Boykins is the smallest player in the NBA. At 7' 5", Yao Ming is one of the tallest. Despite these height differences, both players have success on the court. In Boykins' case, he competes with taller opponents with a mix of speed and strategy. Yao's height lets him tower above many other players to rebound and score.

RIGHT IN THE MIDDLE
At 6' 7" and 222 pounds, Dallas Mavericks forward Michael Finley is one of the most "average" players, size-wise, in the NBA. See the chart on page 65 for more details.

Smallest player in NBA history: Muggsy Bogues, who played from 1987–2001

In 2002 and 2003, Kidd led his New Jersey Nets to the NBA Finals.

Shoe size: 13

Muggsy Bogues, 5' 3"

Jason Kidd, 6' 4"

BIG PLAYER, BIG FAN
Yao Ming and Cuttino Mobley meet a young fan. At 7' 5", Yao casts a rather large shadow over his "regular-sized" fans.

MAGICAL REVOLUTION
At 6' 9", Magic Johnson was the tallest point guard in NBA history. His size and all-around skills helped change the way the game was played. Before Magic, no tall player had possessed the passing skills needed in the position. Magic led the Los Angeles Lakers to five NBA championships in 10 years.

Bol's grandfather was a tribal chief in their native Sudan, and was 7' 10".

Garnett is an excellent ballhandler for such a big player.

Yao Ming's father—another tall Yao—played on competitive basketball teams in China.

Jamal Mashburn is the New Orleans Hornets' top scorer.

Shoe size: 18

Shoe size: 16 1/2

| Jamal Mashburn, 6' 8" | Kevin Garnett, 7' 0" | Yao Ming, 7' 5" | Manute Bol, 7' 7" |

The coaches

EVERY NBA TEAM IS DIRECTED by a coach who wears many hats. He must be a good teacher to show young players the ins and outs of NBA play. He must be a great strategist, planning the plays and tactics to take on each opponent. He must be a good communicator, able to pass on his vision and goals to his team. Head coaches work with assistants and other staff members over a long season; training camps start in October and the season may not end until mid-June. Of course, only the best coaches get to watch their teams play that long. If they're playing in June, it means they're in the NBA Finals.

Auerbach was famous for lighting up a cigar after key victories.

CELTICS GENIUS
Red Auerbach was one of the greatest coaches the NBA has ever seen. He guided the Boston Celtics to nine NBA titles in a 10-year span. When he retired in 1966, he was the winningest coach in league history.

COACHING KING
This signed ball honors the achievement of Lenny Wilkens when, in 1996, he became the first coach in NBA history to surpass 1,000 career wins; he had broken Auerbach's mark of 938 career wins a year earlier. At the time, Wilkens was the coach of the Atlanta Hawks.

Lenny Wilkens
1000th NBA Career Victory
Atlanta Hawks vs. Cleveland Cavaliers
March 1, 1996
Lenny Wilkens

Hand-painted commemorative ball

POINTING THE WAY
A coach can make a big difference during the heated action of a game. Directing his players well can lead a coach and his team to victory. During the 2004 season, Indiana's Rick Carlisle conferred with Jermaine O'Neal.

INDIANA

7

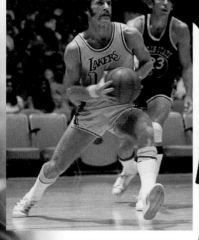

Riley set new standards of fashion on the sidelines, wearing dapper suits and ties to coach games.

PLAYER-TURNED-COACH
Using experience gained as a player is one way to become a great coach. Pat Riley learned all about pro play as a sharp-shooting Lakers guard. Riley has been even more successful as a coach, leading the Lakers to four NBA titles in the 1980s. Riley has also earned the NBA Coach of the Year Award three times, once with the Lakers and later with the New York Knicks and Miami Heat.

PRACTICE MAKES PERFECT
Though far from the spotlight of game time, practice sessions are often where a coach can have the biggest impact. Here, coach Larry Brown works with Allen Iverson at a Team USA practice before the Olympics.

Brown dresses out in sweats for practice, letting him get in the game with his team.

During timeouts, players gather around the coach in the bench area.

THE FUNDAMENTALS
NBA coaches are teachers first. Many started out coaching young players, and still take time to help future stars learn the basics of the game. Here, San Antonio's Gregg Popovich works with a young player at a skills clinic.

Preprinted court diagram

IN THE HEAT OF THE GAME
During timeouts, coaches such as Rick Carlisle diagram plays for their team on dry-erase clipboards like this one. They use special markers to draw lines and symbols.

Youth-size rubber ball

Arenas

KNICKS ON THE MOVE
New York City's Madison Square Garden, home of the New York Knicks, has actually been located in four different places in that city. The arena above was built in 1925 and closed in 1968. The current Madison Square Garden is one of the most famous basketball arenas in the world.

THE ARENAS WHERE NBA TEAMS PLAY have changed as much as the players and the gear. Originally older buildings with few luxuries, arenas today are sleek and modern, with everything from Internet-wired seats to shops, restaurants, and luxury suites. Most teams play in newer arenas that seat about 17,000-21,000 people, though some are larger. But while the arenas are new, the goal for the hometown fans is the same as the old days: Cheer loudly for their favorites in hopes of giving their team a "home-court advantage" that can help them overcome even the toughest opponent.

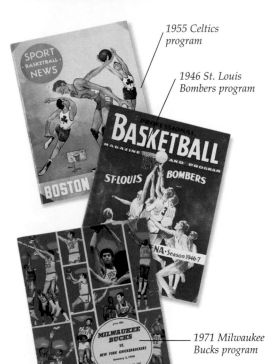

1955 Celtics program

1946 St. Louis Bombers program

1971 Milwaukee Bucks program

This bronze statue of Jordan is 12 feet tall and weighs 2,000 pounds.

HONORING BASKETBALL GREATNESS
Arenas are not only the perfect backdrop for NBA action, they also house memorabilia to honor basketball greats. Unveiled in 1994, this statue of Michael Jordan outside Chicago's United Center is one of the city's most popular tourist attractions. The old Chicago Stadium was equally well-loved, bringing fans treats such as a 1939 Harlem Globetrotters game (ticket, below left).

MEMORY MAKERS
Fans at arenas then and now buy programs for each game that include rosters, team news, statistics, and more. Collectors prize older programs such as these, which feature teams and stars of past NBA glory.

Ticket to see another legend play in Chicago: the Harlem Globetrotters

STATE OF THE ART
Home of the Indiana Pacers, Conseco Fieldhouse opened in 1999 and is one of the NBA's newest arenas. The 750,000-square-foot building cost more than $183 million and was made with more than 600,000 bricks.

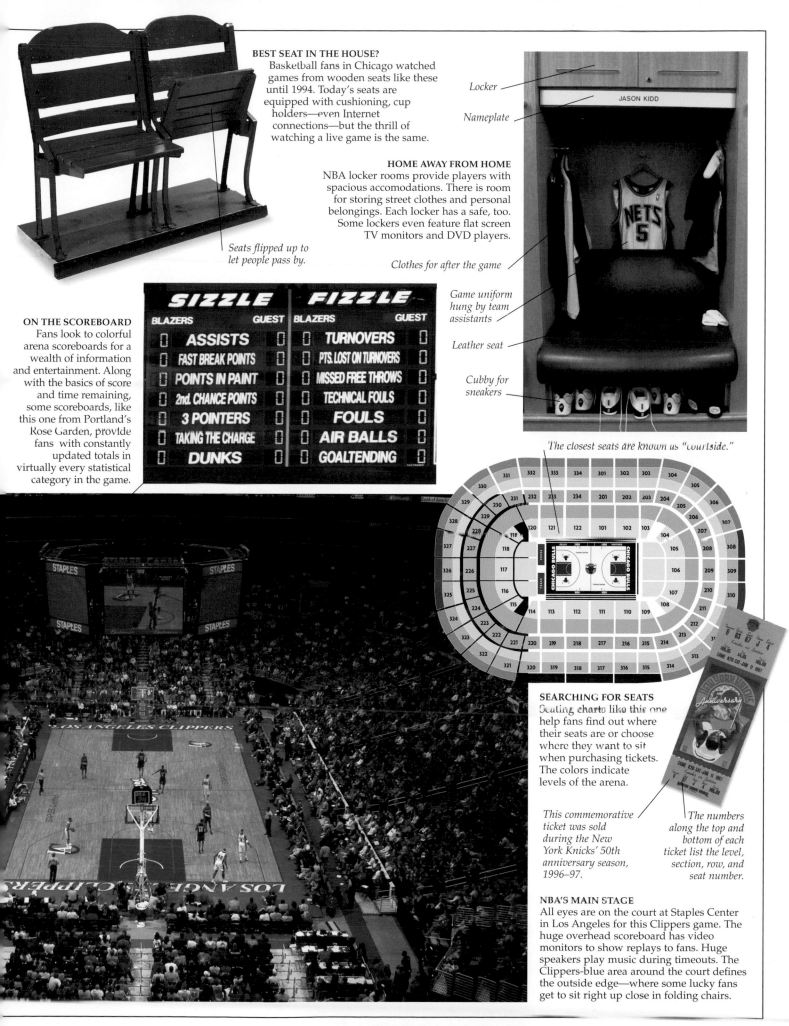

BEST SEAT IN THE HOUSE?

Basketball fans in Chicago watched games from wooden seats like these until 1994. Today's seats are equipped with cushioning, cup holders—even Internet connections—but the thrill of watching a live game is the same.

Seats flipped up to let people pass by.

Locker

Nameplate

JASON KIDD

HOME AWAY FROM HOME

NBA locker rooms provide players with spacious accomodations. There is room for storing street clothes and personal belongings. Each locker has a safe, too. Some lockers even feature flat screen TV monitors and DVD players.

Clothes for after the game

Game uniform hung by team assistants

Leather seat

Cubby for sneakers

ON THE SCOREBOARD

Fans look to colorful arena scoreboards for a wealth of information and entertainment. Along with the basics of score and time remaining, some scoreboards, like this one from Portland's Rose Garden, provide fans with constantly updated totals in virtually every statistical category in the game.

SIZZLE		FIZZLE	
BLAZERS	GUEST	BLAZERS	GUEST
ASSISTS		TURNOVERS	
FAST BREAK POINTS		PTS. LOST ON TURNOVERS	
POINTS IN PAINT		MISSED FREE THROWS	
2nd. CHANCE POINTS		TECHNICAL FOULS	
3 POINTERS		FOULS	
TAKING THE CHARGE		AIR BALLS	
DUNKS		GOALTENDING	

The closest seats are known as "courtside."

SEARCHING FOR SEATS

Seating charts like this one help fans find out where their seats are or choose where they want to sit when purchasing tickets. The colors indicate levels of the arena.

This commemorative ticket was sold during the New York Knicks' 50th anniversary season, 1996–97.

The numbers along the top and bottom of each ticket list the level, section, row, and seat number.

NBA'S MAIN STAGE

All eyes are on the court at Staples Center in Los Angeles for this Clippers game. The huge overhead scoreboard has video monitors to show replays to fans. Huge speakers play music during timeouts. The Clippers-blue area around the court defines the outside edge—where some lucky fans get to sit right up close in folding chairs.

Ready to play

GAME DAY. IT'S WHEN AN NBA player gets to shine. There are 82 games in the 24-week-long regular season, which means a team plays an average of one game every two days. It's a tough schedule, but lots of practice and a regular game-day routine keep players ready to go. The pre-game schedule officially begins with a healthy breakfast, followed by a 10 AM shootaround. Players work up a light sweat before visiting the trainers' room to treat any injuries. Then they head home or to the hotel room for an afternoon of rest. Two hours before tip-off, it's back to the arena to stretch, dress, and get ready to play!

Yao arrives in Atlanta on game day.

ANOTHER DAY, ANOTHER CITY
With 41 away games during a season, teams do a lot of traveling. Charter planes help the journey pass more quickly and comfortably with extra-large seats for these super-sized players. Yao Ming and his teammates pass the time by working on laptops, reading, or catching a nap to help adjust to changing time zones.

A trainer helps Yao with a firm heel hold.

The trainer presses Yao's left leg to help the stretch.

Hamstrings are stretched to prepare for lots of running.

Arms muct be strong and limber to reach for shots and block opponents.

LOCKER HANGOUT
When players arrive at the arena, they head straight to the locker room area to change into their uniforms before the game. Each player has a chair by his locker, so Yao and his teammates relax together for a few minutes and enjoy a laugh to soothe any pre-game nerves.

PREGAME STRETCHING
Stretching exercises are mandatory for all players before practices and games. It's important that players loosen their leg, arm, and back muscles to reduce any tension. Stretching not only helps prevent injuries, but it can also increase performance. Yao stretches before every game to ensure he can move his 7' 5" body and reach peak performance on the court.

PRE-GAME TREATMENTS
Trainers' rooms are often busy before and after games. Some treatments have changed little since the early days of basketball. Others are high-tech, such as this stimulator machine, used to loosen muscles.

Adhesive tabs attach wires to leg.

Padded physical-therapy table

The stimulator machine sends small electric shocks through muscles, helping them relax.

Wires transmit electricity to the body.

PRE-GAME SHOOTAROUND
Players warm up an hour or so before the game. They participate in a variety of shooting drills. Yao likes to work on his low post moves before a game.

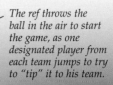

The ref throws the ball in the air to start the game, as one designated player from each team jumps to try to "tip" it to his team.

"A 7' 5" CENTER FROM SHANGHAI, CHINA... NBA ALL-STAR... YAO MING!"
Pregame introductions occur before every tip-off. It's customary to have the visiting team introduced before the home team. Yao greets teammates and ball boys after he is introduced before the hometown Houston fans. The enthusiasm and cheers always give players a boost.

Pressurized finger sleeve

1, 2, 3... GAME TIME!
As part of the pre-game preparation, teams huddle before taking the court. One leader or captain of the team delivers an inspirational message or words of encouragement to his teammates in the huddle. By this time, players are emotionally charged and ready to take the court for the game. The huddle helps them focus their energy and shows team unity.

As his team's tallest player, Yao is often chosen to do the "jump ball."

Each player leaps as high as possible into the air, trying to reach the ball before his opponent does.

TIP-OFF!
After hours of pre-game stretching, shooting, and other warm-ups, the anticipation is finally over. The game is on! Warm-up shirts and pants are peeled off, shoe laces are tightened, and 10 players meet at half court for the tip-off. The referee blows his whistle. It's time to play ball.

47

Courtside

COURTSIDE AT AN NBA GAME IS ALMOST as fast-paced as the action on the court itself. Both team benches are right beside the court and are full of activity as players come in and out of the game, and team assistants work to provide water or warm-up suits. Television and radio broadcasters work from courtside, too, along with dozens of photographers. Cheerleaders and dance teams fill the ends of the court, encouraging fans to yell louder. Perhaps most frenzied are mascots who roam courtside and wander throughout the arena, entertaining fans and providing laughs. During timeouts and at halftime, the courtside action moves to center court, as dance teams and mascots perform.

ARE YOU OK?
Trainers are invaluable members of every NBA team. Along with overseeing the day-to-day health of players, trainers work with injured athletes on rehabilitation and are always ready during games to come to the aid of a player.

ALL ACCESS COVERAGE
From the sidelines during games and the locker room before and after, television broadcasters help fans at home get close to the action. National and local TV covers NBA action extensively. Here, Andre Aldridge of NBA TV interviews LeBron James about a postseason honor.

GO, TEAM, GO!
NBA teams employ dance teams and cheerleaders to entertain fans during timeouts and at halftime. They also encourage fans to cheer for the home team. When not performing, many NBA dance teams go on visits as goodwill ambassadors in the community.

The Laker Girls are one of the NBA's most popular dance squads.

SIDELINE CELEBRATION
Players who are not on the court are still very much a part of the game. Along with helping encourage their teammates from their courtside seats, these players must be ready to get into the game at any moment.

Hugo reaches great heights with the aid of a trampoline.

Showstoppers

NBA teams have costumed mascots that have become almost as well known as the players. They help fans cheer for the home team, perform stunts and tricks on the court during timeouts, and are especially popular with young fans.

Mascots' costumes often include either a team jersey or lots of team color.

The gorilla shows off his ball handling skills to entertain fans.

GOING APE IN PHOENIX
The Phoenix Suns Gorilla is a mascot legend. The athletic simian has had fans going ape since 1980. His humorous exploits and great dunking ability have made him popular around the world, and he has visited Australia, Canada, and China, among other places.

ACROBAT ARTISTS
Many NBA mascots are daring acrobats who perform creative dunks (sometimes with the aid of a trampoline). New Orleans' "Super Hugo" is a three-time NBA Mascot Slam Dunk Champion.

FAN FAVORITES
Plastic or ceramic bobblehead dolls sometimes make an appearance on the sidelines, as teams offer these and other souvenirs as a free gift to fans at special games or events. The dolls have become a popular gametime give-away, and a hot collectible among fans.

NBA Fans

TRUE CELTICS FAN
What better way to cool off at FleetCenter while watching your favorite team? Celtics fans in New England and across the country are some of the most devoted in all of sports.

PASSIONATE. LOYAL. ENTHUSIASTIC. MODERN. Meet the 21st century NBA fan. Perhaps no other sport has such dedicated fans all over the world than basketball. Fans of the NBA in particular can be found in every city in the United States and Canada, cheering on their favorite teams. Millions of them watch their hoops heroes on television or listen to games on local radio. Fans also love the high-energy excitement of attending an NBA game in person; Inside and outside the arena, the atmosphere is electric. Whether they watch on TV or in person, fans go to great lengths to show their support.

HAWK AND A SMILE
Suns fans quenched their thirst with this specially marked pack of Coke featuring Hall of Famer Connie "The Hawk" Hawkins.

ON-COURT PROMOTIONS
Fans of all ages get the chance to strut their stuff during game breaks. Teams host contests like this scooter derby in which fans can win prizes.

SIGN OF THE TIMES—FANS EXPRESS THEIR DEVOTION
Part of the fun of attending an NBA game is expressing yourself. One popular way for fans to do that is by making a sign. Depending on the message, some lucky fans might even be seen on TV holding their special signs.

TRUE COLORS
Dallas Mavericks fans are as passionate as any in the NBA. These young women showcase their artistic creativity and team spirit prior to tip-off. But Dallas isn't the only city to feature such devoted followers. You'll find enthusiastic fans (and painted faces) in every NBA city.

Official replica Mavericks jersey

Numbers for entry into costume contest

Catchings shows young players how to practice dribbling like the pros.

WNBA CLINIC
NBA and WNBA players often host skills clinics for young fans to help them learn the game. These fans are receiving ball-handling pointers from Tamika Catchings of the Indiana Fever.

Official WNBA ball

AUTOGRAPH FRENZY
Fans love collecting autographs of their favorite NBA players. Fans ask players, such as Gary Payton, above, to sign shirts, pennants, basketballs, and more. You name it, they'll sign it (just ask nicely!).

NBA collectibles

A wide variety of products let fans take their love of the NBA home with them. Clothes, souvenirs, items for the home, and multimedia are just some of the possibilities.

JERSEYS, NOW AND THEN
This retro Minneapolis Lakers jersey (shown front and back) recalls the former home of the Los Angeles Lakers. The "old look" uniforms have become a popular way for fans to show support for their favorite teams or players.

Shaquille O'Neal bobblehead doll

Nets mascot (Sly) bobblehead doll

Basketball bowl and glass

Beanbag chair

NBA BOBBLEHEADS
Players, coaches, mascots—everyone is in on the bobblehead craze! These stand-up dolls are popular collectibles. The unique "Celebriducks" are models of NBA players designed as rubber bath ducks.

Allen Iverson Celebriduck

DVD and video game

WE'RE NO. 1
Foam fingers are one of the most popular displays of team loyalty. These oversized souvenirs are sold at NBA arenas and feature the team's logo and colors. Fans wave these fingers at gametime—it's their way of lending a hand!

51

The WNBA

Championship trophy

Holdsclaw demonstrates classic jump shooting form.

WOMEN HAVE BEEN PLAYING BASKETBALL since shortly after it was invented. However, the development of a professional women's league trailed far behind men's leagues. By the 1990s, women's college basketball had grown in popularity, and the 1996 U.S. women's Olympic team brought home the gold. Spurred by their success, the Women's National Basketball Association (WNBA) tipped off in June 1997. The New York Liberty and the Los Angeles Sparks played in the first game. Finally, women had a professional league—and young fans had a host of new role models. Players such as Cynthia Cooper, Sheryl Swoopes, Rebecca Lobo, Lisa Leslie, and Chamique Holdsclaw became household names among hoops fans. Since then, the eight-team league has expanded to 14 teams, while adding new fans of all ages.

Cooper returned to the Comets in 2003 after a two-year retirement.

CYNTHIA COOPER: MS. MVP
Cynthia Cooper was the WNBA's first superstar. The 5' 10" guard led the Houston Comets to four straight championships and won four WNBA Finals MVP awards. Before joining the Comets, Cooper won two NCAA championships with the University of Southern California and earned an Olympic gold medal.

TIMELESS EXCELLENCE
Videos like these feature footage from the regular season and the playoffs. With a record four WNBA titles, the Houston Comets have created an entire library of championship moments.

CAPITAL GAIN
Chamique Holdsclaw was a superstar before she joined the Washington Mystics. The 6' 2" forward led the University of Tennessee to three straight national titles. She won the WNBA's Rookie of the Year Award in 1999.

The official WNBA ball is orange and oatmeal-colored, and slightly smaller than an NBA game ball.

50-FOOT MIRACLE
The celebration was almost underway. The Houston Comets were 2.4 seconds from a third consecutive championship—and the New York Liberty needed a miracle. Down by two points, New York's Teresa Weatherspoon took two dribbles and launched a 50-foot shot that dropped in the basket: Liberty 68, Comets 67.

The game clock shows 0.4 seconds remaining as the shot flies through the air.

The ball floats in a high arc toward the basket.

Teresa Weatherspoon

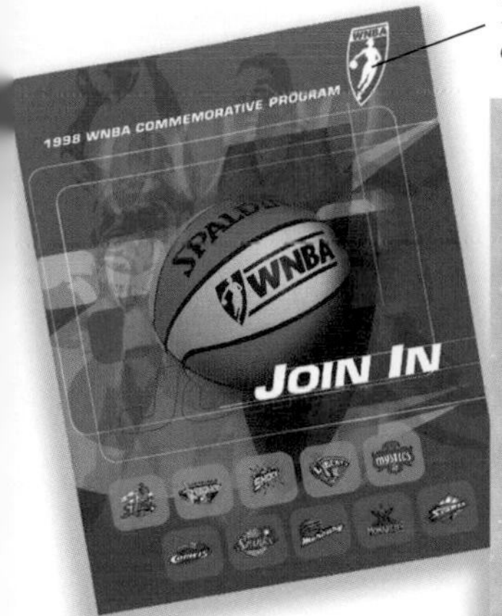

1998 WNBA
commemorative program

Punch-out cards
feature pictures
and information
about each player.

EXTRA! EXTRA!

Programs and card sheets are favorite WNBA collectibles. Spectators who attend regular-season and playoff WNBA games receive souvenirs for free: Teams give away these card sheets at every home game. These oversized cards feature action photos plus the latest roster and statistical info.

Some players wear
tight undergarments
called compression
shorts under their
uniform shorts.

L.A.'S SPARK PLUG

Lisa Leslie is the ultimate winner. The 6' 5" All-Star center has won championships at every level: high school, college, international, and professional. Leslie's high school teammates knew she was destined for greatness when she once scored 101 points— in one half. Leslie starred at USC and has sparked the L.A. Sparks to two WNBA titles.

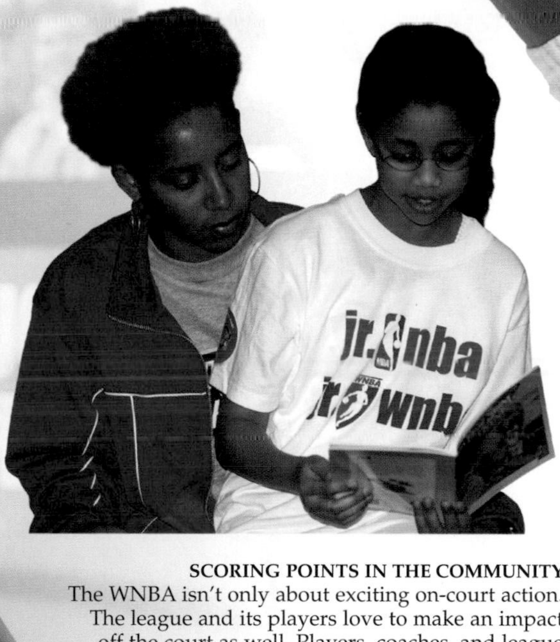

SCORING POINTS IN THE COMMUNITY

The WNBA isn't only about exciting on-court action. The league and its players love to make an impact off the court as well. Players, coaches, and league personnel lend their support to many worthwhile causes, including the Jr. NBA & Jr. WNBA and Read to Achieve programs. The WNBA's Breast Health Awareness Campaign helps raise funds to fight breast cancer, the most common cancer among women.

Plastic and nylon
braces support some
players' ankles.

TAKING THE WNBA BY STORM

Sue Bird's career took flight immediately in the WNBA. The 5' 9" guard turned around the losing ways of the Seattle Storm. Before her pro career, Bird led the University of Connecticut to a perfect 39–0 season and was a key part of two NCAA championship teams.

Team USA

THE UNITED STATES and more than 200 other countries take part in international basketball tournaments, where top players get to compete against teams from other countries. U.S. men's and women's teams are selected by USA Basketball, the sport's governing body, to represent the nation in international play. Since 1989, NBA players have been allowed to join these teams, bringing a new level of talent to Team USA.

FIRST IN FINLAND
Basketball has been a part of every Olympics since 1936. U.S. teams have won a record 11 gold medals, including posting a perfect 8–0 record in 1952.

PAN-AM GAMES
Held every four years, this event features teams from nations in North and South America. This pin is from the 1967 event in Winnipeg, Canada. That year, the U.S. men's team won a gold medal, and the women took silver.

DREAM TEAM PROGRAM
This program features members of the second Olympic "Dream Team," an all-star roster of NBA players. Programs, pennants, T-shirts, and many other souvenirs became hot collectibles as this team won gold again.

1992 DREAM TEAM RECEIVES MEDALS
In 1992, NBA players took part in the Olympics for the first time. Featuring superstars Michael Jordan, Magic Johnson, Larry Bird, and Charles Barkley, the "Dream Team" is considered the greatest collection of basketball talent ever. The team had an average victory margin of 43.8 points and won all eight of its Olympic contests. Here, the team receives its gold medals after defeating Croatia.

Traditional dress from Barcelona, where the 1992 Games were held

Olympic symbol

GOLD MEDAL PERFORMANCE
U.S. women's teams have also had great success in the Olympics. The 1984 team led by Cheryl Miller and Teresa Edwards earned this gold medal at the Los Angeles Olympics. U.S. women's teams have won every gold medal in women's basketball since then.

A TOUCH OF MAGIC

Even though he retired from the NBA in 1991, Magic Johnson was a member of the 1992 Dream Team. He helped win Olympic gold to add to his remarkable achievements, which included championships in high school, college, and the NBA.

International rules do not allow uniform numbers as high as Magic's usual 32, so he wore 15 in 1992.

Though made by a different manufacturer, the ball used in international play has the same weight and dimensions as the one used in NBA games.

Neoprene sleeve to protect an old knee injury

STILL NEED TO PRACTICE

Although members of the national teams are all top-flight players, they still must practice before tournaments to adjust to each other's game and to the flow of international-style competition. Here, LeBron James works out in his Team USA gear in preparation for playing in the 2004 Summer Olympic Games in Athens, Greece.

USA Basketball logo

1996 OLYMPIC TICKET

The second Dream Team romped to victory in 1996 in Atlanta, winning the gold medal by defeating Yugoslavia in the final. This ticket, like all Olympic tickets, has become a hot souvenir.

1996 Team USA logo

Clothing company logos and size label

1996 TEAM JERSEY

John Stockton of the Utah Jazz wore this jersey in 1996. He was one of the few players to participate in both the 1992 and 1996 Olympics.

CLOSING THE GAP

While the U.S. continues to be the home of the most top pro players, countries around the world are improving rapidly, and American domination of international play is being challenged. This U.S. team took part in the 2004 Summer Olympics, but did not make the finals. Argentina defeated Italy for the gold medal.

Global game

FROM A HUMBLE START in a Massachusetts YMCA, basketball has spread around the globe. It is played in every country in the world, and fans watch pro leagues in dozens of nations. Each year, more and more players from those leagues join the NBA, helping maintain its status as the world's top basketball league. As evidence of the NBA's popularity, more than 200 nations tune in to watch the Finals, and half of NBA.com's users live outside the U.S.

1996 Lithuanian team Olympic jersey

1972 USSR team pennant

OLYMPIC ACTION
In addition to pro leagues, many international players shine in the Olympics. Arvydas Sabonis played for his home country of Lithuania in the 1992 and 1996 Games. Before joining the NBA, Sabonis also played basketball in the Soviet Union.

FIBA is the international governing body of basketball.

FOR GREAT CONTRIBUTIONS
The International Basketball Federation (FIBA) gives this medal during its Congress, held every 10 years, to individuals who make great contributions to international basketball.

YAO MING
NBA history was made on June 26, 2002, when the Houston Rockets made Yao Ming of China the first number-one overall draft pick to come from an international basketball league.

YAO MING FANS
Many Asian-American fans have taken to attending Yao Ming's games, sporting signs that cheer him on in his native language.

Drazen Petrovic played for the Nets from 1989 to 1993.

GLOBAL SURFING
The NBA now boasts fans in nations around the world. One of the ways they keep up with their favorite teams and players is through NBA.com, which features pages customized in many languages, including French (above), Chinese, Japanese, Spanish, and German.

TONI GOES FOR TWO
Before joining the NBA in 1993, sweet-shooting, 6' 11" forward Toni Kukoc (7) helped Yugoslavia and then Croatia win silver medals in the Olympics. Kukoc is one of several NBA players to represent his home country in the Summer Games.

Toni Kukoc of the Croatian National Team drives to the basket at the 1996 Olympic Games in Atlanta.

DRAZEN PETROVIC
Sharp shooter Drazen Petrovic of Croatia was one of the first international superstars to make the jump to the NBA. Sadly, he was killed in a car accident in 1993. For his many successes in the sport, he was elected to the Hall of Fame in 2002.

FROM BELGRADE TO THE BIG TIME
A native of Belgrade, Yugoslavia, Peja Stojakovic has become a star in the NBA for the Sacramento Kings. The 6' 9" forward has played on several All-Star teams and is one of the top shooters in the league. Before joining the Kings in 1998, he played three seasons in the Greek professional league. In 2002, he helped Yugoslavia win the World Championship title.

NBA goes to Japan

The NBA Japan Games are another example of the global spread of the game of basketball. Five times during the 1990s, NBA teams played regular season games in Japan, the only nation outside North America to enjoy such action. NBA players and officials were overwhelmed by the enthusiastic response of Japanese fans. More than 66,000 people attended a pair of games in 1999. In 2003, the L.A. Clippers and the Seattle SuperSonics participated in the Japan Games.

JAPANESE FANS
Thousands of fans turned out to watch the game—and show their love of basketball—when the NBA visited Japan to play a regular season game in 1999.

NBA JAPAN GAME
More than 32,000 fans packed the Tokyo Dome for the opening tip-off of the 1999–2000 season. The Minnesota Timberwolves took on the Sacramento Kings in a two-game series.

Fans appeal to the broadcasting station to get on TV.

READ ABOUT IT IN JAPANESE
Hoop, the NBA's official monthly magazine featuring player profiles, stats, and news, is translated into Japanese for fans in Japan.

2003 All-Star Game logo

NBA All-Star Game

THE FIRST ALL-STAR GAME
The first all-star contest was played in Boston in 1951 and hosted by Boston Celtics owner Walter Brown (center). "Easy" Ed McCauley (22) was the MVP of the game. Celtics star Bob Cousy (14) also played for the home crowd.

THE ANNUAL NBA ALL-STAR GAME features teams made up of the best players from the Eastern and Western Conferences, playing in an entertaining showcase that is often an exciting and high-scoring affair. Since the game does not count in the standings, many players have the opportunity to show off some of their more creative offensive skills. The first game was held in 1951, after NBA public relations director Haskell Cohen was inspired by baseball's similar mid-season contest. In 1984, the Slam Dunk and Three-Point contests were added, making All-Star a full weekend of events. The All-Star Game itself is now the culmination of a week-long celebration of basketball.

EMPIRE ALL-STARS
This is the program from the 1956 game won by the West over the East. The game was the only NBA All-Star Game ever played in Rochester, New York.

ALL-STAR RING
Each player who took part in the 1984 All-Star Game in Denver received a ring like this one. The East team won 154-145 in overtime, setting an All-Star record for most points.

Seattle skyline on 1987 ticket

TICKETS 1987
All-Star Game tickets are some of the most sought-after in the sports world. All-Star Saturday events include the popular Slam Dunk and Three-Point contests.

1967 JERSEY
NBA great Wilt Chamberlain was a 13-time All-Star. He wore this jersey during the 1967 game, held in San Francisco. That city's Golden Gate Bridge is featured on the front.

SLAM DUNK ACTION
All-Star Games usually feature many amazing individual plays, as players use the game as a stage for great performances. In 1986, Ralph Sampson, the Rockets' 7' 4" center, rose above his East Division opponents to make this awesome slam.

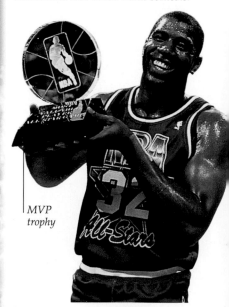

MVP trophy

MAGICAL MOMENT
Magic Johnson stole the show at the 1992 All-Star Game in Orlando. Three months earlier, Johnson had announced his retirement after being diagnosed with HIV. The NBA legend returned to action in the All-Star Game, leading all scorers in the game with 25 points and earning the game's MVP honors.

Bill Russell

Wilt Chamberlain

Bill Walton

David Robinson

Kevin McHale

Oscar Robertson

NBA AT 50

In 1996, the NBA celebrated its 50th anniversary (dating to the founding of the Basketball Association of America). A panel of experts selected the 50 greatest players in NBA history. These players had a combined 107 championships and nearly one million points. Forty-seven of the top 50 gathered for this historic photo at the 1997 All-Star Weekend.

THREE-POINT CONTEST
One of the highlights of All-Star Saturday is the Three-Point contest. The shooting exhibition features the NBA's most accurate shooters. Steve Kerr won the title in 1997.

SLAM DUNK CONTEST
The NBA Slam Dunk contest, which began in 1984, features the league's premier leapers. Dunkers display their creativity and athleticism in front of judges. Fred Jones (pictured above) was the champion in 2004.

MR. ALL-STAR
San Antonio Spurs forward/center Tim Duncan is a regular member of All-Star teams. The two-time NBA MVP was named the co-MVP of the All-Star Game in 2000. He is shown here leaping for a dunk in 2003.

NBA Finals

SINCE THE FIRST NBA FINALS WAS HELD IN 1947, the winners of the NBA title have formed a select group of athletes representing the top of their game. Once a year, the winners of the Eastern and Western Conference titles meet in the best-of-seven NBA championship series to decide who will join those championship ranks. The Lakers have taken part in 27 Finals, the most ever, and have won 14 times. The Celtics own the most NBA championships, with 16, including eight in a row from 1959 to 1966. Since 1969, a Finals MVP has been named. Michael Jordan of the Chicago Bulls won six MVP awards, the most ever.

THE ULTIMATE PRIZE
The Larry O'Brien NBA Championship Trophy is awarded to the winner of the NBA Finals. Created in 1978, the trophy was named for Larry O'Brien, the NBA's third commissioner, in 1984.

Dial-style game clock in the old Boston Garden

A MAGICAL PERFORMANCE
One of the greatest games in NBA history was played by Magic Johnson of the Lakers in the 1980 Finals. Though only a 20-year-old rookie guard, he took the place of injured All-Star center Kareem Abdul-Jabbar in Game 6. Magic dominated the game, scoring 42 points and grabbing 15 rebounds. The Lakers defeated the 76ers and won the NBA title.

THE ULTIMATE CHAMPION
No one owns more NBA championship rings than Bill Russell. The Hall of Fame center led the Boston Celtics to 11 titles in 13 seasons, eight of them consecutive. Russell was a premier defensive player who was also both player and coach for two of Boston's championship seasons.

BULLISH CELEBRATION
Chicago fans swarm the United Center court moments after the Bulls clinch the 1997 NBA title. Celebrating championships became a familiar scene in Chicago during the 1990s. The Bulls won six titles in eight seasons and clinched the title with victories at home three times.

BACK-TO-BACK RINGS
Players who win NBA titles receive jewel-studded gold rings like these given to Houston Rockets players after they won in 1994 (far right) and 1995. The 1995 ring features diamond replicas of the team's two Larry O'Brien trophies.

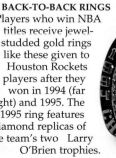

Hakeem Olajuwon hoists the trophy during a 1994 parade.

DRESS LIKE A CHAMP
T-shirts, hats, and other NBA championship apparel is premade in two versions—for both possible outcomes—so that the right one is available immediately after the final game ends.

VICTORY PARADE
After a team wins the NBA championship, it can usually expect to enjoy a victory parade attended by tens of thousands of cheering fans in its home city.

FINALS HIGHLIGHTS
NBA videos and DVDs help fans relive their teams' greatest moments. Available soon after the Finals end, the tapes include season highlights and great moments from the Finals.

2003-2004 Pistons' NBA title DVD

Basketball Hall of Fame

BASKETBALL'S HIGHEST INDIVIDUAL HONOR is a place in the Naismith Memorial Basketball Hall of Fame. Named for James Naismith, the game's inventor, and located in Springfield, Massachusetts, where he created basketball in 1891, the Hall of Fame recognizes the best that the game has to offer. All levels of basketball are honored here, including players from the amateur, professional, and international ranks. The Hall of Fame also recognizes coaches, referees, members of the media, and other men and women who have contributed to the sport. A handful of teams have also been named to the Hall.

Program from the first NBA season

OLD-TIME PROGRAMS
The Hall of Fame contains a large library of printed material relating to the game. These programs, from original NBA teams in Rochester, St. Louis, and Washington, D.C., are just some of the thousands of game and team programs in the Hall's archives.

Local businesses often sponsored programs with ads like this one.

This dome houses the Honors Ring—a collection of artifacts from every inductee, and the centerpiece of the Hall of Fame.

WHERE IT ALL BEGAN
The first class of inductees was named to the Hall of Fame in 1959 and included Dr. James Naismith, George Mikan, and the Original Celtics. The first Hall of Fame building was opened in 1968 in Springfield, Massachusetts, to house basketball artifacts and honorees' plaques.

The surface of the dome, made of high-tech fiberglass, is covered with 800 lights that can blink in more than six million different sequences of color and movement.

BASKETBALL WONDER
Today's Basketball Hall of Fame building opened in 2002. It contains more than 80,000 square feet of museum and exhibit spaces, all devoted to basketball. Exhibits feature basketball memorabilia and artifacts. There is a theater that shows a film of the history of basketball and 13 interactive video programs. After learning all about basketball's greatest, visitors can head to "Center Court" to test their own basketball skills on a regulation NBA court.

THE F. MASON CUP

In 1912, Edward Wachter of the Troy Trojans was the MVP of the old New York State League and received this silver trophy, now part of the Hall's collection. Wachter was elected to the Hall of Fame in 1961.

"100-Point Game"

Chamberlain's autograph, uniform number, and game date

RECORD-SETTING SHOES

Wilt Chamberlain wore these sneakers in 1962 when he became the only player to score 100 points in a game.

Basketball model

This tower is 15 stories tall.

Inductee's name

RING OF HONOR

Hall of Fame inductees receive rings upon their enshrinement. This ring was given to George Mikan, a member of the Hall's first class in 1959.

This quote refers to Willis Reed's appearance in the 1970 NBA Finals.

FAMOUS ANNOUNCERS EXHIBIT

Most fans get their news of NBA games from radio and TV announcers, some of whom—Johnny Most, Chick Hearn, Marv Albert—have become broadcasting icons. This exhibit lets fans hear these announcers call famous plays from NBA history.

GIVE IT A SHOT

Visitors to the Hall can get some hands-on experience at this shooting exhibit. They face large cutouts of players from the NBA and WNBA. The new Hall building features several such interactive exhibits that let fans experience, in a small way, what it's like to play the game.

SUPER DRIBBLER

Many experts consider Globetrotters star Marques Haynes the greatest ball-handler and dribbler in the sport's history. Haynes was named to the Hall as a player in 1998.

Team owner Manny Jackson

Harlem Globetrotters

Though not a part of the NBA, the Globetrotters are an important part of basketball history. Formed in 1927, they evolved from a top competitive team to the entertainers they are today.

GLOBAL APPEAL

The "'Trotters" have played in more than 20,000 games in more than more than 115 countries. This poster advertises a game they played in Japan.

TROTTERS INDUCTED

The Harlem Globetrotters were inducted into the Hall of Fame in 2002.

Did you know?

FASCINATING FACTS

Mark Price is the NBA's all-time free-throw percentage leader. The former All-Star point guard, who played nine seasons for the Cleveland Cavaliers, shot .904 (2,135–2,362) in 12 seasons in the NBA. Hall of Famer Rick Barry ranks second with a .900 (3,818–4,243) percentage, which he accomplished over a 10-year NBA career.

Only three men have been enshrined twice in the Naismith Memorial Basketball Hall of Fame (as both players and coaches): John Wooden, Lenny Wilkens, and Bill Sharman. As a player, Wooden led Purdue to a national title in 1932, and as a coach, he guided the UCLA Bruins to a record 10 NCAA titles. Wilkens was a nine-time All-Star point guard who went on to great heights as a coach. Sharman was a top player and coach for Boston.

Joe Dumars guarded by Larry Bird

Magic Johnson has the three highest single-game assist totals in NBA Finals History with 21, 20, and 20 again. He is also the NBA Finals leader in career assists with 584 and career steals with 102. Johnson was the NBA's all time assists leader before John Stockton of the Utah Jazz eventually surpassed him.

The NBA team in Utah can thank another city for its nickname. The Jazz originally played in New Orleans, home to that type of music.

The closest finish in the race to become the season scoring champion came in the 1977–78 season. George Gervin of the Spurs scored 58 points in the final game to overtake David Thompson of the Nuggets.

 Kareem Abdul-Jabbar set an NBA record by scoring 1,000 or more points in 19 consecutive seasons. The six-time NBA champion and five-time NBA MVP is the NBA's all-time leading scorer.

The NBA named Joe Dumars of the Detroit Pistons the recipient of the first-ever NBA Sportsmanship Award. The NBA Sportsmanship Award is a major award that is presented annually to an NBA player who best represents the classic ideals of sportsmanship on the court. The trophy is also named after the former Piston, who played 14 seasons in Detroit, amassing more than 16,000 points and helping lead his team to two NBA titles.

 Wang Zhizhi—not Yao Ming—was the first Chinese player to compete in the NBA. The 7'0" center played in his first NBA game as a member of the Dallas Mavericks in the 2000-01 season. Wang scored six points and grabbed three rebounds in a 108-94 win over the Atlanta Hawks.

Wilt Chamberlain, who owns the single-game record for most points with 100, also owns the mark for the second highest mark with 78, which he also accomplished as a member of the Philadelphia Warriors. The "Big Dipper" has actually posted six of the top 10 all-time single-game scoring performances.

Wilt was part of the longest winning streak in NBA history. The Lakers won 33 straight games from November 5, 1971 through January 9, 1972. The streak was ended by the Milwaukee Bucks, then led by Kareem Abdul-Jabbar. The Lakers went on to set a record (since topped) with 69 victories in the season, on their way to the NBA championship.

No Boston Celtics player has ever won a scoring title yet the team has an NBA record 10 MVP Award Winners.

Stockton prepares to make a bounce pass.

John Stockton

John Stockton is the NBA's all-time leader in total assists with 15,806 and total steals with 3,265. Only Magic Johnson's 11.2 assists per game were greater than Stockton's 10.5. The 10-time All-Star guided the Jazz for 19 seasons and helped lead Utah to back-to-back NBA Finals appearances. The No. 16 overall pick in the 1984 NBA Draft out of Gonzaga University, Stockton was named as one of the 50 Greatest Players in NBA History in 1996.

In 1972 Wayne Embry became the first African-American General Manager in professional sports when he was assumed those duties with the Milwaukee Bucks. Before making history, Embry was an NBA All-Star, having played 11 seasons with the Cincinnati Royals, Boston Celtics, and Milwaukee Bucks. He was also a member of the '68 Celtics championship team.

In game two of the Eastern Conference semifinals in 2001, Allen Iverson of the 76ers (54 points) and Vince Carter of the Raptors (50 points) put on an unprecedented and unmatched scoring binge. For the first time, two opposing players scored at least 50 points each in a playoff game. Iverson's teammates added more than Carter's did, however, and Philadelphia won this impressive game.

Wilt Chamberlain

QUESTIONS AND ANSWERS

Q What was the longest game in NBA history?

A On January 6, 1951, the Indianapolis Olympians defeated the Rochester Royals 75-73 in six overtimes.

Q What was the highest-scoring game in NBA history?

A The Detroit Pistons defeated the host Denver Nuggets 186-184 in triple overtime on December 13, 1983. The game featured 12 players reaching double-figures in scoring (with only two three-pointers!), including Detroit's Isiah Thomas (47 points), John Long (41), and Kelly Tripucka (35), as well as Denver's Kiki Vandeweghe (51), Alex English (47), and Dan Issel (28).

Q What NBA players have scored 70 or more points in a game?

A David Robinson (71 in 1994), David Thompson (73 in 1978), Elgin Baylor (71 in 1960), and Wilt Chamberlain (six times in his career) have all hit 70 plus.

Q What is the most prolific father-son scoring combination in NBA history?

Alex English

A Hall of Famer Rick Barry (18,395 points in his NBA career) has combined with sons Brent, Jon, and Drew for more than 29,000 points (and counting, thanks to Brent and Jon still playing). Another Hall of Fame father, Dolph Schayes, totaled 28,027 points with son Danny, who enjoyed an 18-year NBA career.

Q Have NBA players gotten bigger over time?

A They haven't gotten much taller, but thanks to advances in weight training, they have gotten larger and heavier. See the chart at right to see how much NBA players have grown.

Rick Barry

Q Who was the first woman to dunk in a professional basketball game?

A All-Star center Lisa Leslie of the Los Angeles Sparks grabbed the attention of the basketball and sports world with her one-handed jam in the first half against the Miami Sol at STAPLES Center in Los Angeles on July 30, 2002.

Q Who played in the most NBA Finals games?

A Boston Celtics legend Bill Russell played in 70 games. The 12-time All-Star is the NBA's ultimate winner, leading the Celtics to 11 titles in 13 seasons.

Q What odd thing happened on November 4, 1994, in San Antonio?

A A Spurs game was delayed due to rain...sort of. An indoor sprinkler system went off by accident. It took an hour to clean up the mess, but the game eventually went on.

Q What was the greatest NBA championship team of all time?

A You'll get a debate from fans of other teams, and there probably isn't a right answer, but some experts point to the Chicago Bulls of 1995–96, who won an all-time record 72 games in the regular season on their way to their fourth NBA title.

Q Which teams once played in other cities with the same nickname?

A The Pistons (Fort Wayne), the Hawks (a.k.a. the Tri-Cities Blackhawks, at Iowa and Illinois border, along the Mississippi River; Milwaukee, St. Louis), the Lakers (Minneapolis), the Warriors (Philadelphia, San Francisco before the Golden State), the Clippers (San Diego), the Nets (New York), the Kings (Omaha, Kansas City), the Jazz (New Orleans), the Rockets (San Diego), the Hornets (Charlotte), and the Grizzlies (Vancouver), each had different addresses before their current ones.

Lisa Leslie

Q What was the longest shot in pro basketball history?

A Look to the American Basketball Association, which merged with the NBA in 1976, for this answer. On November 15, 1967, Jerry Harkness's Indiana Pacers trailed the Dallas Chapparals 118-117 with just seconds left. Harkness got the ball near his own end line and launched the ball nearly the length of the court. It went in the basket! His 92-foot shot (the court is only 94 feet long) will probably never be topped. Oh, yes, it also gave Indiana the one-point win and Harkness a place in history.

The growth of the NBA player

The average NBA player has grown surprisingly little in the past two decades. This chart lists league averages in size, age, and years of NBA experience.

YEAR	HEIGHT	WEIGHT (LBS)	AGE	EXP.
1989–90	6' 7.09"	214.82	26.79	3.95
1990–91	6' 7.16"	216.16	27.01	4.08
1991–92	6' 7.04"	216.47	27.09	4.20
1992–93	6' 7.06"	219.86	27.19	4.15
1993–94	6' 7.34"	221.68	27.26	4.28
1994–95	6' 7.19"	221.50	27.43	4.56
1995–96	6' 7.27"	223.66	27.56	4.42
1996–97	6' 7.20"	223.67	27.74	4.63
1997–98	6' 7.11"	222.95	27.82	4.82
1998–99	6' 7.10"	222.85	27.82	4.81
1999–00	6' 7.26"	224.68	27.95	5.20
2000–01	6' 7.03"	223.47	27.75	5.01
2001–02	6' 7.26"	224.05	27.47	4.82
2002–03	6' 7.40"	225.40	27.34	4.73

Brent Barry

Who's who?

IN 1996, A PANEL OF EXPERTS comprised of media, former players and coaches, current and former general managers, and team executives selected the 50 Greatest Players in NBA History. Given the number of players who have left their mark on the game over the years, it was a very difficult process for this blue-ribbon panel. Out of the hundreds of greats who have played the game, here are the 50 greatest:

KAREEM ABDUL-JABBAR
When Abdul-Jabbar left the game in 1989 at age 42, no NBA player had ever scored more points, blocked more shots, won more MVP awards, played in more All-Star Games, or logged more seasons. He was a Rookie of the Year, member of six NBA championship teams, six-time NBA MVP, two-time NBA Finals MVP, and a 19-time All-Star.

NATE ARCHIBALD
"Tiny" Archibald became the only player to lead the league in both scoring and assists in a season (34.0 ppg, 11.4 apg in 1972–73).

PAUL ARIZIN
Paul Arizin burst into the league in 1950 with a daring new weapon: the jump shot. By the time Arizin was leading the league in scoring in 1952, only a few other players had mastered the shot.

CHARLES BARKLEY
One of four players in NBA history that have compiled 20,000 points, 10,000 rebounds, and 4,000 assists (along with Abdul-Jabbar, Chamberlain, and Karl Malone), Barkley also stood out for the entertaining, sometimes outrageous commentary on basketball and life he provided.

Charles Barkley

RICK BARRY
Barry is the only player ever to lead the NCAA, NBA, and ABA in scoring. His name appears near the top of every all-time offensive list. He scored more than 25,000 points in his professional career and was named to 12 All-Star teams.

ELGIN BAYLOR
Those who saw Baylor play can easily recall his great all around skills. "He was one of the most spectacular shooters the game has ever known," said Baylor's longtime teammate Jerry West in 1992.

DAVE BING
The speedy Bing amassed 18,327 points in 901 contests (20.3 ppg). In only his second season, 1967–68, he led the NBA in scoring. Bing would quietly go on to off-court success as a self made industrial magnate.

LARRY BIRD
For 13 seasons with the Celtics, this superstar personified hustle, consistency, and excellence in all areas of play—as a scorer, a passer, a rebounder, a defender, a team player, and, perhaps above all, as a clutch performer.

WILT CHAMBERLAIN
He was the most awesome, unstoppable offensive force the game has ever seen. Dominating the game as few players in any sport ever have, Chamberlain seemed capable of scoring and rebounding at will, despite the double- and triple-teams and constant fouling tactics that opposing teams used to try to shut him down.

BOB COUSY
Cousy, one of the greatest passers and playmakers in NBA history, was flashy before flashy was cool. Cousy helped build the Celtics of the 1950s and 1960s into basketball's most enduring dynasty—America's team.

DAVE COWENS
Cowens earned a berth in the Basketball Hall of Fame because of his tenacity and work ethic as a mainstay of the Celtics in the 1970s, leading the team to NBA Championships in 1974 and 1976.

BILLY CUNNINGHAM
Cunningham played fiercely, coached intensely, and won frequently. As a player and then a coach for the 76ers, he was part of two NBA championship teams.

DAVE DEBUSSCHERE
A hard-nosed, tenacious forward, DeBusschere was one of the game's best-ever defenders. He was named to the NBA All-Defensive First Team in each of the award's first six years of existence.

CLYDE DREXLER
One of the game's all-time great guards, "The Glide" was known for his high-flying swoops to the basket. A perennial All-Star and a member of the 1992 U.S. Olympic "Dream Team," Drexler twice led the Blazers to the NBA Finals and later helped the Rockets win an NBA title.

JULIUS ERVING

Julius Erving

"Dr. J" was the dominant player of his era, an innovator who changed the way the game was played. He was a wizard with the ball, performing feats never before seen: midair spins and whirls punctuated by powerful slam dunks. A dignified and disciplined man, Erving was the epitome of class and an ideal ambassador for the game.

EARVIN "MAGIC" JOHNSON
Few athletes are truly unique, changing the way their sport is played with their singular skills. "Magic" was one of them, combining ball-handling skills with size in a new and marvelous way. He led the Lakers to five NBA championships.

PATRICK EWING
One of the finest shooting centers, he left the game as the Knicks' all-time leader in nearly every category and the game's 13th all-time scorer with 24,815 points.

WALT FRAZIER
Frazier presided over the Knicks for 10 years from 1967 to 1977. As a Knicks player, Frazier played in seven NBA All-Star Games, and was named to four All-NBA First Teams.

GEORGE GERVIN
Only Chamberlain and Jordan have won more league scoring championships than "The Iceman's" four, and Gervin was the first guard ever to win three titles in a row.

HAL GREER
Over the course of 15 NBA seasons Greer averaged 19.2 points per game, racking up 21,586 points (14th on the all-time list). He was an All-Star for 10 straight seasons and the second-leading scorer on Philadelphia's vaunted title team of 1966–67.

JOHN HAVLICEK
Known for clutch performances in big games, Havlicek posted impressive numbers during his illustrious 16-year career. His 26,395 career points make him he Celtics' all-time leading scorer.

ELVIN HAYES
Few athletes are truly unique, changing the way their sport is played with their singular skills. Hayes was one of them, a revolutionary player who, at 6'9", was the tallest point guard in league history.

SAM JONES

Called "Mr. Clutch" by many of his peers, Jones was one of the linchpins of the fabulous Boston juggernaut of the 1950s and 1960s. His uncannily accurate bank shots, lightning quickness, and cool demeanor helped the Celtics win 10 NBA Championships.

MICHAEL JORDAN

He is called the greatest basketball player of all time. A phenomenal athlete with a unique combination of grace, speed, power, artistry, improvisational ability and an unquenchable competitive desire, Jordan single-handedly redefined the NBA superstar. He won 10 scoring titles and led the Bulls to six NBA titles.

JERRY LUCAS

Lucas wasn't particularly tall or bruising, nor was he a great leaper, but his name can be found at the top of any list of great rebounding forwards in NBA history.

KARL MALONE

"The Mailman" won two MVP awards (1996–97 and 1998–99), 14 All-Star selections, and 11 All-NBA First Team selections. He also became the second leading scorer in the history of the game.

MOSES MALONE

One of the game's all-time great centers, Malone was a relentless rebounder and effective scorer in his 21 years. He is the third-leading rebounder and fifth-leading scorer in NBA history.

PETE MARAVICH

"Pistol Pete" was a spectacular showman who helped open up the game of basketball in the 1970s. Maravich wasn't the first player to dribble behind his back or make a between-the-legs pass, but his playground moves and hot dog passes were considered outrageous during his era.

KEVIN MCHALE

With his incredibly long arms and legs, McHale used his physical gifts to excellent advantage during his 13-year career with the Celtics, becoming one of the best inside players the game has ever seen.

GEORGE MIKAN

Mikan, a 6'10" giant of a man, with his superior coordination and fierce competitive spirit, was one of the prototypes for the dominating tall players of later decades.

EARL MONROE

"Earl the Pearl" Monroe was a dazzling ballhandler and one-on-one virtuoso who made crowds gasp with his slashing drives to the hoop.

HAKEEM OLAJUWON

During his 18-year career, Nigerian-born Olajuwon became one of the greatest players in NBA history. He had a storybook season in 1993–94 when he became the first player to be named NBA MVP, Defensive Player of the Year, and Finals MVP in the same year.

SHAQUILLE O'NEAL

The youngest player named to this list, the 7'1", 300-pound O'Neal is simply one of the most dominant big men in the history of the game, bringing size, strength, and skill that have rarely been seen in a single package. He helped the Lakers win three titles.

ROBERT PARISH

A 7'1" center with strength, agility, and remarkable endurance, Parish won three NBA titles with the Celtics in the 1980s He played in an NBA-record 1,611 games.

BOB PETTIT

This tall, thin forward was deemed too slight at 200 pounds to survive the pounding of an NBA season. But he did succeed, and after 11 years, he retired having become the first player in the league to top 20,000 points.

SCOTTIE PIPPEN

A talented scorer and rebounder, Pippen was a six-time NBA champ with the Bulls.

WILLIS REED

In Game 7 of the 1970 NBA Finals, Reed authored one of the ultimate examples of leadership and dedication, playing despite a severe leg injury to lift the Knicks to an emotional championship.

OSCAR ROBERTSON

The "Big O" is the player against whom all others labeled "all-around" are judged. In 1961–62, just his second season in the league, he averaged a triple-double for an entire season.

John Paxson and Isiah Thomas

David Robinson

DAVID ROBINSON

"The Admiral" was a marvel player and a respected figure off the court. He won Rookie of the Year, NBA MVP, and Defensive Player of the Year awards, plus helped the Spurs win two NBA titles.

BILL RUSSELL

Russell was the cornerstone of the Celtics dynasty of the 1960s, an uncanny shotblocker who revolutionized NBA defensive concepts. A five-time NBA Most Valuable Player and a 12-time All-Star, he helped the Celtics win nine NBA titles.

DOLPH SCHAYES

Schayes was one of professional basketball's early superstars, a crack shooter and top rebounder whose career stretched from the NBA's inaugural year in 1948 to basketball's emergence as a major sporting attraction in the early 1960s.

BILL SHARMAN

Sharman still ranks among the top free-throw shooters of all time with an .883 lifetime percentage. In an 11-year NBA career played mostly with the Celtics, Sharman was voted to the All-NBA First or Second Team seven times.

JOHN STOCKTON

Perhaps the best passer in NBA history, Stockton left the game holding the career assist mark (15,806). He also retired as the all-time steals leader with 3,265. His Jazz team made the playoffs in each of his 19 seasons.

ISIAH THOMAS

"Zeke" was one of the greatest "small men" ever to play pro basketball. Barely over six feet, he was a feisty competitor who helped the last-place Pistons rebound to win back-to-back NBA champions (1989–1990).

NATE THURMOND

Thurmond was one of the all-time great NBA centers. The Hall of Famer played 14 professional seasons in the 1960s and 1970s, posting career averages of 15.0 points and 15.0 rebounds per game.

WES UNSELD

A 6-7 bull of a center, Unseld forged his reputation on relentless rebounding, bone-jarring picks, and laser-beam outlet passes. He was the league's MVP and Rookie of the Year in 1968–69 and later captained the Bullets to four NBA Finals appearances in the 1970s and to a championship in 1977–78.

BILL WALTON

After winning three straight College Player of the Year Awards, Walton had a fine pro career. With the Trail Blazers, he was 1977–78 league MVP.

JERRY WEST

Combine a deadly jump shot, tenacious defense, obsessive perfectionism, unabashed confidence, and an uncompromising will to win, and you've got West, one of the greatest guards in NBA history. He was an All-Star every year of his career and led Los Angeles to the NBA Finals nine times.

LENNY WILKENS

After a Hall of Fame career as a player, Wilkens turned to coaching and led his teams to more wins than any other coach in NBA history.

JAMES WORTHY

"Big Game James" was a member of three NBA championship teams with the Lakers and was the 1988 Finals MVP.

Find out more

IF YOU'RE INTERESTED IN LEARNING more about basketball, there are plenty of opportunities out there to do so. Want to get in the game? All you really need to play is a ball and a hoop, but organized leagues are often as close as your school or your community's recreation center. There you can learn the game and play with people of all age groups. Talk to a physical education teacher to help you find a team. Fans can also learn more about the game, its history, and today's top stars by visiting arenas and special exhibits or on the Internet.

TIME FOR TIP OFF
Many teams hold camps or clinics to help kids learn to play. Under the eye of NBA players, kids at this special basketball camp hosted by the Seattle Supersonics start a game with a tip-off.

LOOK, MOM, WE WON!
Fans get to see NBA's championship trophies close at hand when the statues go on tour. These Detroit Pistons fans pose with their team's NBA trophies during the 2004 Championship Tour.

USEFUL WEB SITES

- **www.nba.com**
  Official National Basketball Association site
- **www.wnba.com**
  Official Women's National Basketball Association site
- **www.nbdl.com**
  Official National Basketball Developmental League site
- **www.hoophall.com**
  Official Naismith Memorial Basketball Hall of Fame site
- **www.usabasketball.com**
  Official page for USA Basketball, the national governing body for men's and women's basketball in the United States
- **www.fiba.com**
  Official International Basketball Federation page
- **www.nbastore.com**
  NBA's online store

NBA ON THE ROAD
When the NBA Jam Van comes to your town, one of the interactive exhibits lets visitors compare the size of their hands to that of NBA stars. Do you have the hands to play in the NBA or WNBA? Find out at the Jam Van.

WHERE THEY PLAY
The Mavericks play here at the American Airlines Center in Dallas, Texas. The players' locker rooms here are among the plushest in the league, with each locker boasting personal video monitors. At this and other NBA arenas, public tours allow fans to go behind the scenes.

NAISMITH MEMORIAL BASKETBALL HALL OF FAME, SPRINGFIELD, MASSACHUSETTS
The town in which the sport was created plays host to the game's ultimate shrine, in which professional, collegiate, and amateur legends are all honored. Memorabilia and hands-on exhibits are everywhere (see pictures of memorablia and pictures of an exhibit on this page, plus read more about the Hall on pages 62–63).

NBA STORE, NEW YORK, NEW YORK
The premier shopping destination for all professional basketball fans is located in the heart of New York's legendary Fifth Avenue in midtown Manhattan. Everything from notebooks to jackets to autographed goods is available for fans of every NBA team

NBA CITY, ORLANDO, FLORIDA
On the grounds of Universal Studios in Orlando, Florida, this is the ultimate theme restaurant for basketball fans, featuring an impressive NBA store as well.

MADISON SQUARE GARDEN, NEW YORK, NEW YORK
They call this New York City home of the Knicks and the WNBA's Liberty "The World's Most Famous Arena." And with so many important and historic events having hapened there, it's hard to argue.

UNITED CENTER, CHICAGO, ILLINOIS
On display at the home of the Chicago Bulls are the team's six glittering, golden NBA championship trophies.

AIR CANADA CENTRE, TORONTO, ONTARIO
The Toronto, Ontario, Canada, home of the Toronto Raptors, is one of the NBA's outposts in the north.

NBA JAM VAN, NATIONWIDE
Watch for the NBA Jam Van to come to a city near you. The NBA Jam Van is a huge, 18-wheel truck that transforms into 8,000 square feet of free basketball and interactive off-court activities. Make slam dunks, play video games, watch great NBA highlights, and more. Visit www.nba.com to see the Jam Van schedule.

SHOOTIN' AT THE HALL
Springfield, Massachusetts is the birthplace of Basketball—and the home of its Hall of Fame. The Hall includes a full-size basketball court where visitors can pretend they're being guarded by real NBA and WNBA greats as they take shots. Other interactive exhibits let guests compare their height and sneaker sizes to NBA players.

SHORT SHORTS
At the Basketball Hall of Fame, check out old basketball gear like these satin shorts from the 1940s. The players used leather or canvas belts to help hold up the shorts, which were much shorter than today's versions.

TAKE A SEAT
At the Hall of Fame, take a seat like fans did in the old days. These fold-down wooden seats were once filled with fans cheering on the Boston Celtics at the old Boston Garden.

Glossary

AIR BALL Sarcastic term to describe a shot that doesn't touch the rim

ALLEY-OOP PASS A pass thrown to a player who is running toward the basket. The receiving player leaps, catches the ball in midair, and dunks it or lays it in before he lands.

ASSIST A pass that leads directly to a basket

BACKCOURT A team's defensive half of the court; as it refers to players, a team's guards

BACKDOOR PLAY A fundamental basketball play in which one player passes to a teammate in the high post, and when the defenders follow the ball, another player cuts to the basket from the opposite side of the court to take a pass for an open shot

BANK SHOT A shot that is aimed at a spot on the backboard so that it caroms, or "banks," into the basket

BASELINE The line at each end of the court, under each basket; also: endline

BENCH Reserves

Bench

BOUNCE PASS A pass that bounces on the floor on its way from one player to another

BOX OUT The use of one's body to stay between an opponent and the basket and thus get into better position for a rebound

BRICK A hard, errant shot that bounces wildly off the basket or backboard

BUNNY An open, uncontested shot, usually a layup or dunk; also: snowbird

BURY Sink (a shot), as in "bury a jumper"

CAROM To bounce or rebound off a surface, especially at an angle

CHARGING A violation in which an offensive player runs into a stationary opponent

COAST-TO-COAST From one end of the court to the other

CUT A quick move by an offensive player, usually toward the basket, to get into position for a shot

DEAD-BALL FOUL A foul committed while the clock is stopped and the ball is not in play

DOUBLE DRIBBLE A violation in which a player dribbles the ball, holds the ball, then begins to dribble again

DOUBLE-TEAM The defensive tactic of two players guarding one

DOWNTOWN Far from the basket, often synonymous with beyond the three-point arc

DRAFT The annual selection process by which NBA teams select players from the colleges and elsewhere

DRIBBLE Bounce the ball on the floor

DUNK A shot thrown downward through the basket, with one or two hands; also: slam, slam-dunk, jam

FAST BREAK A play in which a team gains possession and then pushes the ball downcourt quickly, hoping to get a good shot off before the other team has a chance to set up on defense

FIELD GOAL A basket, worth either two or three points, depending on whether it was taken from inside or outside the three-point line (set at 22 feet from the basket)

FLAGRANT FOUL Unnecessary and/or excessive contact committed against an opponent

FOUL A violation, usually, illegal contact between two players

FOUL TROUBLE When a player is nearing the limit for personal fouls before he is ejected from the game, or a team is nearing the limit in each period after which all fouls become shooting fouls. In the NBA, six personal fouls means a player cannot play for the rest of the game.

The ball be above the rim when the shot is taken.

FREE AGENT A player not under contract to any NBA team because his contract has expired or was terminated by his team in accordance with NBA waiver procedures, or because he was eligible for an NBA Draft and was never signed to an NBA contract

FREE THROW An uncontested shot from 15 feet, worth one point. A player who is fouled while in the act of shooting receives two free throws. Also: foul shot.

 Dunk

FRONTCOURT A team's offensive half of the court; as it refers to players, a team's center and forwards

GIVE-AND-GO A fundamental play in which one player passes to a teammate, then cuts to the basket to receive a return pass for an open layup or dunk

GOALTENDING A violation in which a player interferes with a shot while the ball is on its downward arc, pins it against the backboard or touches it while it is in an imaginary cylinder above the basket; may be committed by either an offensive or defensive player

GUNNER A frequent shooter

HAND-CHECKING A violation in which a defender uses his hand to impede a player's progress

HANG TIME The amount of time a player stays in the air while attempting a shot

HIGH POST The area around the free throw circle

HOOK SHOT A shot taken with a sweeping, hooking motion; may be taken while the shooter is stationary or in motion

HOOP Basket or rim; also slang for playing basketball

J Jump shot

JUMP BALL When a referee starts the game or restarts play after opposing teams gain simultaneous possession of the ball. After the teams are realigned, the referee tosses the ball up between two players, who attempt to tap it to a teammate.

JUMP HOOK A hook shot taken while jumping, popular among big men because it is difficult to block

JUMP SHOT A shot taken after a player jumps in the air

LANE The painted area between the end line and the free-throw line near each basket, outside which players line up for free throws. Also known as the key, because in the early years it was key-shaped. It was twice widened to its present rectangular shape.

LOOSE-BALL FOUL A foul committed while neither team has possession of the ball, as while going for a rebound

LOW POST The area at the base of the foul lane to either side of the basket

NET A pass thrown by a player after getting a rebound to a teammate, generally near midcourt, to start a fast break

OUTLET PASS A pass from a player taking a defensive rebound to a teammate to start a fast break

OVERTIME A five-minute extra period that is played when the game is tied after four quarters. If a game remains tied following an overtime period, another is played and another until there is a winner.

PENALTY SITUATION When a team has committed more than its allotted four fouls per quarter and thus each subsequent foul becomes a shooting foul

PICK When an offensive player frees a teammate for a shot by establishing a stationary position that prevents a defensive player from guarding the shooter. If the player who is "setting a pick" is not stationary and contact is made with a defender, it is an offensive foul and his team loses possession of the ball. Also: screen.

PICK-AND-ROLL A play in which an offensive player sets a pick, then "rolls" toward the basket and takes a pass from a teammate for an open shot

PIVOT The area near the basket, generally where the center operates, or the act of changing directions by keeping one foot planted on the ground while stepping in one or more directions with the other foot. Players can hold the ball while pivoting without incurring a traveling penalty.

POST *see* Low Post

POINT GUARD Usually a team's primary ballhandler and the player who sets up the team's offense

POWER FORWARD The larger of a team's two forwards, whose duties generally involve rebounding as much as scoring

PRESS Guard very closely

PUMP FAKE A fake in which a player motions as if he is going to shoot the ball but holds back, hoping his defender will jump out of position

QUADRUPLE-DOUBLE An extremely rare (it's only happened four times in NBA history) achievement in which a player accumulates doubles figures in four of the following categories in the same game: points, rebounds, assists, steals, and blocked shots

REBOUND Gather in and gain control of a missed shot; also: a missed shot that is retrieved

REJECTION A blocked shot

ROCK Ball

Jump shot

SAG A defensive tactic in which a player drops off his man to help double-team a player in the pivot

SCREEN Pick

SHOT CLOCK The 24-second clock used to time possessions. A team must attempt a shot that at least hits the rim within 24 seconds or else it loses possession of the ball.

SIXTH MAN A team's primary reserve, the first substitute to enter a game

SKY-HOOK A hook shot in which the ball is released while the shooter's hand is at the top of the arc; used most effectively by Kareem Abdul-Jabbar, the NBA's all-time career scoring leader

STEAL To take the ball away from an opposing player, either while he is dribbling or by picking off a pass

SWITCH When teammates exchange defensive assignments during play

TECHNICAL FOUL The penalty for a violation of conduct, such as abusive language or fighting. Each technical foul awards a free throw to the opposing team and also means an automatic fine for the player who commits the violation.

THREE-POINT SHOT A field goal worth three points, taken from beyond an arc that is 22 feet from the basket

THREE-SECOND VIOLATION An offensive player may not stand in the lane for three seconds

360 To get away from a defender by doing a complete spin, making a 360-degree turn

TIP-IN To tip a missed shot into the basket

TRAILER An offensive player who trails on a fast break but is often in good position to score after the first wave of defenders goes by

TRANSITION The movement from offense to defense, or vice versa, when the ball changes hands

TRAVELING A violation in which a player takes too many steps without dribbling the ball; also: walking

TURNOVER Loss of ball, either through an errant pass or dribble or an offensive foul

WEAK SIDE The side of the court away from the ball

ZONE DEFENSE A defensive tactic in which players guard areas of the court, rather than specific men. It's illegal in the NBA, but often used in college or high-school basketball.

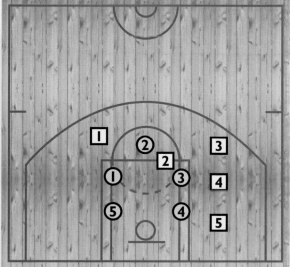

Zone defense (green circles)

Index

Acknowledgments

The NBA, the publisher, and the producers of this book extend very special thanks to the Naismith Memorial Basketball Hall of Fame.

Shoreline Publishing Group would like to thank writer John Hareas for all of his hard work; Beth Hester of DK for her patience and attention to detail; and designer Diana Catherines, who came off the bench to hit a buzzer-beating shot.

The NBA would like to extend special thanks to Paul Hirschheimer. Also to John Doleva, Paul Lambert, Mike Brooslin, Robin Deutsch, and Matt Zeysing of the Naismith Memorial Basketball Hall of Fame.

Basketball court diagrams were created by Milos Orlovic of DK. Original basketball rules photograph on page 6, bottom left, is courtesy Ian Naismith.

Photography Credits:

All photos in this book were provided through Getty Images/ NBA Entertainment. Individual photographers or sources are noted below; photos not listed separately are courtesy NBAE.

(t: top; b: bottom; c: center; l: left; r: right)

Ray Amati: 45tr, 46tl. AP/World- wide: 30tr. Brian Bahr: 59tl, bl. Bill Baptist: 26cl; 39tr; 41tl; 43tr; 46tr (2), bl; 47tl. Gary Bassing: 14r. Andrew D. Bernstein: 20lc; 22bc; 24bl (2); 25r; 27t; 34tl; 35lc; 36br, tr; 38cr; 39lc; 46cr, br; 50cr; 53r; 59b, t, r. Lisa Blumenfeld: 13c. Nathaniel S. Butler: 26tl; 52br; 55br; 56c. Lou Capozzola: 37br. Rich Clarkson: 60bl. Jim Cummins: 31l. Scott Cunningham: 15cr; 56bl. Jonathan Daniel: 17c; 61t. Tim DeFrisco: 41br. Stephen Dunn: 41tr. Allen Einstein: 16c; 43bl. Garrett Ellwood: 13tr; 25bc; 38c; 47lc, r; 52tr. D. Clarke Evans: 43br. Sam Forcenich: 11t, l, bl, br; 45c; 48bl. Greg Foster: 42cl. Steven Freeman: 7bl; 8t, tl, cl; 9 (4 old baskets); 10c, cr; 14tl, b(3); 15t; 16l, bc, tr; 17tr, tc; 18tl, bl; 30cr; 45tl; 54tl, lc, b; 55c, cr; 56cl; 63t (3), cr, br. Jesse D. Garrabant: 19tl; 21l; 23c; 46cl; 55tr. Barry Gossage: 19br; 49bl. Noah Graham: 8r; 20bl; 45b; 51tl. Don Grayston: 27bl; Otto Greule, Jr.: 48tr. Kent Horner: 20br; 50c. Walter Iooss, Jr.: 22tl; 24r; 25tl; 30c; 32br; 33bc; 34cr, bl; 60c. Glenn James: 22r; 50b. George Kalinsky/Major League Graphics: 32l. Mitchell Layton: 12c. Ken Levine: 13br. Andy Lyons: 40tr. Fernando Medina: 18bl; 20r; 37l; 38bl. Donald Miralle: 48b. Ron Modra: 19bc. Robert Mora: 26cr. Layne Murdoch: 26bl; 41bl; 49tr. Joe Murphy: 19bl; 22bl. Naismith Memorial Basketball Hall of Fame: 6 (all except bl); 7t, r, br, c; 10tr; 12tl; 28c, br, tl; 29tl, bl; 44tl; 58tr; 62b; 63bl; NBA Photo Library: 29tr; 30br. Hy Peskin: 21br. Tom Pidgeon: 22tr. Dan Piszczatowksi: 52tl. Jennifer Pottheiser: 8bl; 12c, tr, bc; 16br; 17bl, bc; 18tl, c, br; 25cr; 28bc; 29br (3); 30tr, br; 32tr, cr; 33c, b (4); 34tr, bc, br; 35tl, tc, br; 36tl; 37tr (2); 39br (4); 42bl; 44cl (3); 49br; 50tl (2); 51bl (3); 52tl (3); 54tr; 56tl (2); 57br; 58cl, c, cr, bl; 60br; 62tr (3); 63br. Mike Powell: 54c; 55l. Dick Raphael: 33tr. Ken Regan: 30bl. Jeff Reinking: 51tr; 56tr. Wen Roberts: 43tl. Shem Roose: 53bl. Ezra O. Shaw: 52bl. David Sherman: 40br; 48c. Robert Skeoch: 40bc. Kent Smith: 27br, bc. Noren Trotman: 35tr. Rocky Widner: 18tr; 20tl, 21tr; 40l; 42cr; 57t.

Jacket Credits:

Front cover: tc: Jennifer Pottheiser Getty/NBA Entertainment; cl: Jennifer Pottheiser Getty/NBA Entertainment; tcl: Andrew D. Bernstein NBAE/Getty Images; c: Nathaniel S. Butler NBAE/ Getty Images; cr: Courtesy of the NBA. *Back cover:*c: Nathaniel S. Butler NBAE/Getty Images.